50 MATHEMATICAL PUZZLES AND PROBLEMS

RED COLLECTION

**From the International Championship of Mathematics
Fédération Française des Jeux Mathématiques**

Gilles Cohen, Editor
Éditions POLE

Key Curriculum Press
Innovators in Mathematics Education

Éditions POLE

Coordinator: Michel Criton
Translators: Jean-Christophe Novelli, Elizabeth Terrien
Editor: Gilles Cohen
Reading and Editing Committee: Julien Cassaigne, Francis Gutmacher, Jon Millington,
   Bernard Novelli, Jean-Christophe Novelli, Lucien Pianaro
Problem Authors: Jean-Claude Bartier, Henri Camous, Bernard Chevalier, Florence Cochet,
   Gilles Cohen, Michel Criton, Nicolas Didrit, François Glineur, Francis Gutmacher,
   Jean-Louis Legrand, Patrice Lucas, Sergio Moreno, Bernard Novelli, Yves Rayer,
   Michel Raynaud, Zbigniew Romanowicz, Dominique Souder, Pascalyves Souder

Key Curriculum Press

Project Administrator: Heather Dever
Editorial Assistant: Kyle Bridget Loftus
Mathematics and Translation Reviewer: Dudley Brooks
Production Editor: Jennifer Strada
Copy Editor: Margaret Moore
Production Director: Diana Jean Parks
Production Coordinator: Laurel Roth Patton
Compositor: Laurel Roth Patton
Cover Designer: Caroline Ayres
Prepress and Printer: Malloy Lithographing, Inc.

Executive Editor: Casey FitzSimons
Publisher: Steven Rasmussen

Key Curriculum Press, 1150 65th Street, Emeryville, CA 94608, 510-595-7000
editorial@keypress.com
http://www.keypress.com

Éditions POLE, 31 Avenue des Gobelins, 75013 Paris, France

Printed in the United States of America
10 9 8 7 6 5 4 3 2 1   05 04 03 02 01
ISBN 1-55953-500-8

❖ PREFACE ❖

The International Championship of Mathematics and Logic has been held in France by the FFJM (Fédération Française des Jeux Mathématiques) for more than ten years. Writers for these championships have generated over a thousand original puzzles, which are regularly gathered and published in French by Éditions POLE. Key Curriculum Press is pleased to be able to offer a selection of these problems, translated into English.

The problems are organized by difficulty in three collections: the *Green Collection* (grades 6 through 12), the *Orange Collection* (grades 9 through 12), and the *Red Collection* (grade 9 through college level). Full solutions are provided in each book.

We hope you will enjoy these problems. We invite you to participate with the 150,000 other contestants in the International Championship of Mathematics and Logic, which is held once a year in France. For more information, please write to:

FFJM, 1 Avenue Foch, 94700 Maison-Alfort, France

As you work these problems, keep in mind the essential goals of the championship: to apply reasoning more than knowledge, and to find not only one but all of the solutions to a problem.

Éditions POLE

Key Curriculum Press

❖ CONTENTS ❖

Chapter 4 ❖ Arithmetic and Combinatorics

Chapter 5 ❖ Equations and Systems

Chapter 6 ❖ A Matter of Logic

CHAPTER I

Measures in the Plane

1 ❖ The Shortcut

Every morning, when I leave home, I walk to the nearest bakery to buy some muffins. I usually walk down two wide, straight avenues. They intersect at right angles at O, with $OA = 57$ meters and $OB = 43$ meters. But if I'm late, I take a shortcut through the alley at $\overline{MN}$. When I enter the alley, either at M or N, I've already covered a third of the way.

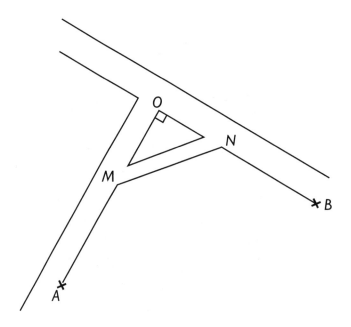

❖ How many meters do I save with this shortcut?

2 ❖ Doubloon Island

Erik the Logical was quite a pirate. He sailed the Caribbean Sea for 15 years and gathered a big treasure, which he stashed on Doubloon Island. Shortly before dying, he gave his son instructions on how to find his treasure:

"On the island, there's a huge rock (R) and an ancient tree (T), one kilometer apart. The treasure is at the vertex of a triangle that has one side lying somewhere on segment TR and an angle of 30 degrees at vertex R. One side of the triangle is 600 meters and another is 400 meters. . . ."

Alas! He died before saying anything else!

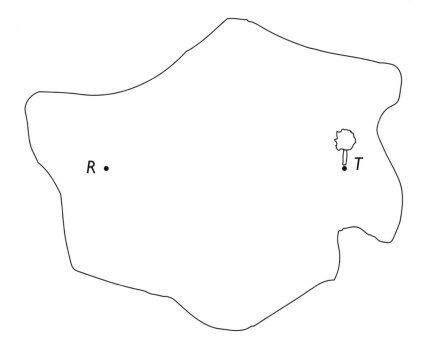

❖ Locate the possible sites of the treasure on the map above.

Note: We checked and the treasure was not at *R!*

---

3 ❖ Parallels

Mr. Tejada asked his students to cut a parallelogram from a piece of cardboard: "I want it to have a height of 7 centimeters, a side of 14 centimeters, and a diagonal of 37 centimeters," he said.

At the next class, he was surprised to see that four of his pupils had found different figures.

Julia and Annabel had drawn different parallelograms, but the figures had the same area, and Vincent and Julius had found two other parallelograms. Mr. Tejada was quite confused when Vincent said that his parallelogram had an area that was twice the area of Julius's.

"Let's see," he said. "It seems true, but it's not really true."

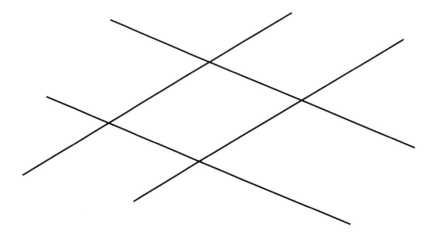

❖ How long would the diagonal of Vincent's parallelogram have to be so that it has an area equal to exactly twice the area of Julius's parallelogram, without changing the other dimensions? Give the exact value, using radicals if necessary.

50 Mathematical Puzzles and Problems ◆ *Red Collection*
©2001 Key Curriculum Press

4 ❖ Planet of the Games

On the Planet of the Games, everyone loves to play games. Of course, among the 12,000 inhabitants, some like card games better, some are enthusiastic about chess, and others just love dice games. Yet everyone practices everything, and harmony (there are also those who play the piano) is all around.

The planet flag accurately symbolizes the distribution of the population according to their favorite hobbies. It is parallelogram-shaped, and each zone represents one game, its area being proportional to the number of people who play that game. The gray zone represents the number of people who like math games.

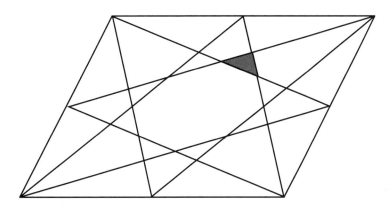

❖ How many people like math games?

Note: The vertices of the star-shaped polygon are the vertices of the parallelogram and the midpoints of its sides.

5 ❖ Cake Walk

Matthew is visiting his friends at Tania's house *(T)* and wants to take them out for dessert. They're about to go to Math's Chinese Bakery *(M)* when Matthew realizes that stopping by Logico's Ice Cream Parlor *(L)* first would add only 1,996 paces to their walk.

Between Tania's house, the bakery, and the ice cream parlor, the roads are straight, and the triangle *TLM* has a right angle at *L*. The triangle's sides can be measured in an integral number of paces.

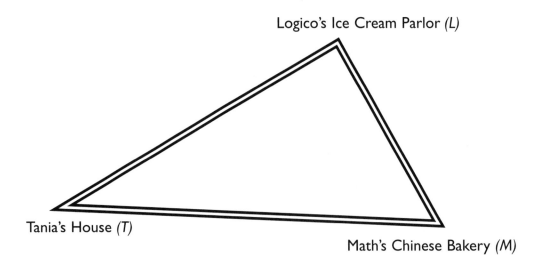

Logico's Ice Cream Parlor (L)

Tania's House (T)

Math's Chinese Bakery (M)

❖ Knowing that they don't walk more than 10,000 paces, find the number of paces between Tania's house and Math's Chinese Bakery.

6❖Polly and the Nonagon

In the Gone family, everyone is very fond of geometric constructions using rulers and compasses. Each child has his or her favorite polygon. Polly (the eldest) has just discovered a stonecutter's recipe in an old book, describing how to build a regular nonagon (nine-sided polygon).

> Draw a circle with center O and radius 10 centimeters.
> Draw two perpendicular diameters, $\overline{AB}$ and $\overline{CD}$.
> Draw an arc with center A and radius AO intersecting the circle at E.
> Draw an arc with center B and radius $\overline{BE}$ intersecting $\overrightarrow{OD}$ at F.
> Draw an arc with center F and radius $\overline{FA}$ intersecting $\overleftrightarrow{CD}$ at G.
> Draw an arc with center C and radius $\overline{CG}$ intersecting the circle at H.
> Use the distance CH, duplicate it on the circle eight times, and connect the nine points thus obtained.

Polly hurries off and draws the polygon as described . . . but then doubt strikes her!

❖ Is Polly Gone's polygon really regular? If not, how great is the error in taking $\overline{CH}$ as the side of a regular nonagon? Give your answer as a percentage, rounded to the nearest tenth of a percent.

You can use:

$$\sqrt{2} \approx 1.41421$$
$$\sqrt{3} \approx 1.73205$$
$$\sqrt{5} \approx 2.23606$$
$$\sin 20° \approx 0.34202$$
$$\sin 40° \approx 0.64278$$
$$\cos 20° \approx 0.93969$$
$$\cos 40° \approx 0.76604$$

7❖Mona and Lisa's Fields

Mona and Lisa's fields are triangles, neither of them equilateral. All sides of both triangles measure whole numbers of hectometers.

Two sides of Mona's field have the same length as two sides of Lisa's field. The three angles of Mona's field are equal to the three angles of Lisa's field. The area of Mona's field is smaller than that of Lisa's field.

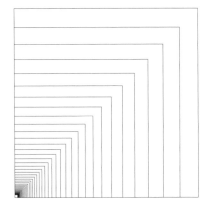

❖ What is the minimum perimeter of the smaller field (in hectometers)?

CHAPTER 2

The Plane and Affine Space

8 ❖ Gene's Swimming Pool

Eugene has an octagonal swimming pool. Its eight sides are, consecutively, 10 meters, 20 meters, 30 meters, 40 meters, 50 meters, 60 meters, 70 meters, and 80 meters long. All the pool's angles are right angles.

❖ What is the surface area of Gene's pool in square meters?

9 ❖ The Discrete Theorem

Discrete 3-space is the three-dimensional space in which every point has integral coordinates. Francis claims to have found the smallest number n of different points that must be chosen in this space in order to be sure that among all the possible triangles, at least one has a circumcenter (center of gravity) whose coordinates are whole numbers.

❖ What is the value of n?

> *"A discrete set is a set that is seen and not heard."*

10 ❖ Five with One Blow

Mathematica has been captured by the dreadful Logicos, who wishes to test Mathematica's reasoning ability. She is locked in a room, and the only door unlocks in a special way: 32 tricolored circular dials, which can only be turned clockwise, have their red sectors facing down. The door opens only when the 32 dials have their white sectors facing down.

But the mechanism has some rules:

- Each time, five dials must be turned together (they don't have to be adjacent).
- Each dial can be turned only 120 degrees at a time.

As soon as one of these rules is broken, the door is locked forever.

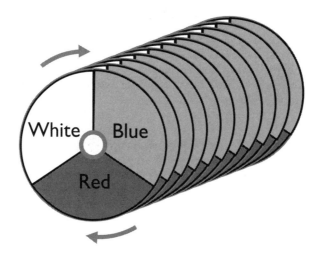

❖ What is the minimum number of steps needed for Mathematica to open the door?

11 ❖ A Little Bit of Cutting Up

Cut up the figure into four parts of exactly the same size and shape.

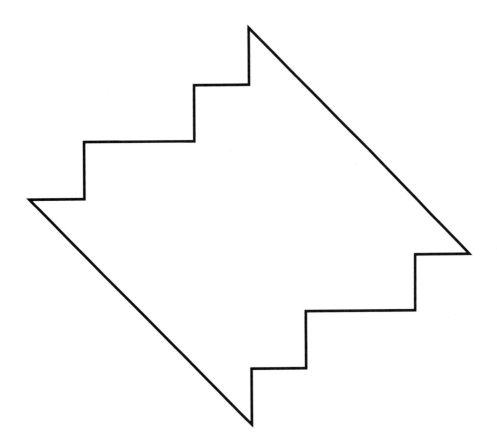

12 ❖ Soaking It Up

A semi-circular sponge (seen from above in the illustration) has a diameter of 20 centimeters. The sponge, full of detergent, slides (without being squeezed) on the floor in the corner of a room, keeping both *A* and *B* in contact with the walls at all times.

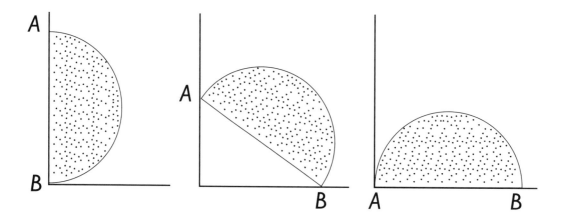

❖ What is the area that will be washed? Give your answer in square centimeters, rounded to the nearest integer if necessary.

50 Mathematical Puzzles and Problems ◆ *Red Collection*
©2001 Key Curriculum Press

13 ❖ Net Volume

A cardboard box is tetrahedral. Cut it along the three edges from a vertex, and lay the faces flat on the table; you will obtain a net of the tetrahedron. This net is a square, the sides measuring 30 centimeters.

❖ What was the volume of the original box?

14 ❖ Sweet Tetrahedron

A cube of sugar candy is cut with a saw to obtain a tetrahedron. The tetrahedron's vertices are the centers of four faces of the original cube. The volume of the candy (as a tetrahedron) is 9 cm³.

❖ What is the volume of sugar that was removed?

15 ❖ A Crystal Ball?

To predict the future, Claire Voyant uses a very curious crystal "ball," which she describes in the following manner:

- When it is lit from above, its shadow projected onto a horizontal plane situated below it is a perfect circular disk.
- When it is lit from the right, its shadow projected onto a vertical plane situated to its left is a perfect circular disk identical to the first.
- When it is lit from the front, its shadow projected onto a vertical plane situated behind it is a perfect circular disk identical to the two others.

Furthermore, of all the objects having these characteristics, it is the one that has the largest volume.

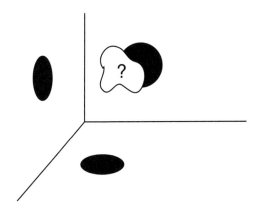

❖ How many faces (not necessarily planar) does Claire's crystal "ball" have?

CHAPTER 3

Trigonometry

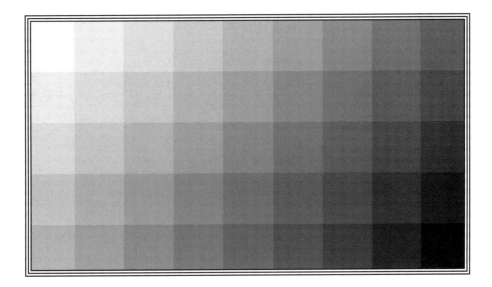

16 ❖ The Angle-Scraping Machine

Angela has built a strange machine with thin metal rods, as shown below. Except for the two longer rods, all of the rods are the same length.

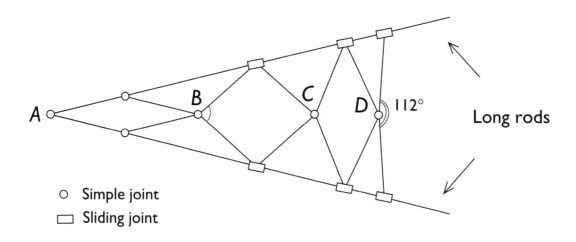

○ Simple joint
▭ Sliding joint

❖ Find the value in degrees of the indicated angle of B when the indicated angle at D is 112 degrees.

Note: The angles in the figure are not accurate.

17 ❖ The Legacy of Circulus

Circulus, the well-known imaginary Roman emperor, wants to apportion his sumptuous property between his four children—three sons and a daughter. The property is in the form of an equilateral triangle with 8 kilometers on a side. From every vertex of this triangle there is a straight road to the opposite side. Each son's share is a triangle, with one side coinciding with a side of the property and the other sides skirting a road. The daughter's share is also a triangle, every side of which skirts a road. (In the figure, the dotted lines indicate the prolongation of the roads.) Circulus wants each of his children to be able to fit out a "circus" (a circular arena) in the interior of that child's portion. These arenas, destined for games, must all have the same radius.

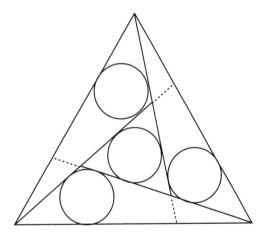

❖ What is the largest this radius can be? Give the radius rounded to the nearest meter.

You can use $\sqrt{2} \approx 1.414$, $\sqrt{3} \approx 1.732$, $\sqrt{5} \approx 2.236$, and $\sqrt{7} \approx 2.646$.

18 ❖ Sinuous

Find the minimum value of n for which the expression $\sin 2^n$ has the greatest possible value, where n is a positive integer and 2^n is the measure of the angle in degrees.

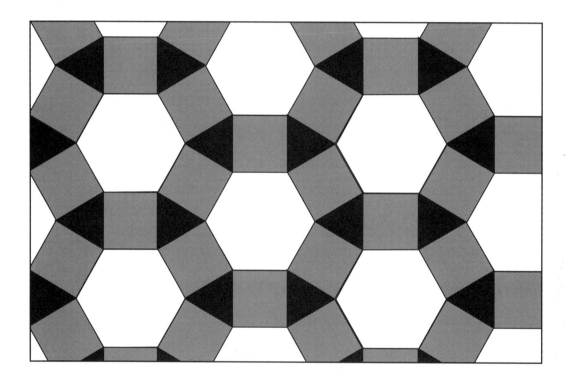

19 ❖ Mathematica's Jewels

The famous pirate Kursouf is out looking for a renowned treasure, Mathematica's jewels. He who owns all the jewels is granted absolute wisdom!

This most feared pirate has managed to get his hands on a map of the Isle Under Time. The map includes the instructions of Mathematica's husband Erik the Logical, who buried the jewels there himself before dying.

According to the map, the jewels are situated at the vertices of all the triangles *ABC* that fulfill these conditions:

- One vertex is at *A* and another is elsewhere on the Boardwalk.
- Angle *B* measures 60 degrees.
- Side *AC* measures 7 kilometers.
- The sum of the other two sides is 11 kilometers.
- The vertices are on the island.

Kursouf is cunning, but not a very skilled geometer, so he has decided to kidnap you before leaving for the Isle Under Time. Watch out for the sharks in the Endless Ocean if you don't find all of Mathematica's jewels!

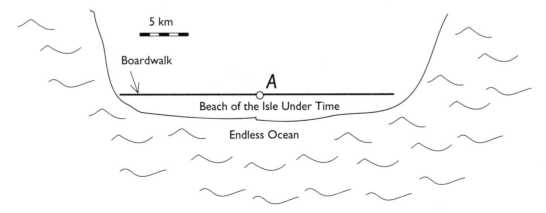

❖ State the number of jewels and mark their location on the map.

20 ❖ Daphne's Daffodils

Daphne, the gardener, was asked to plant six daffodil bulbs, meeting these conditions:

- No three bulbs among the six can be in line.
- Among all the possible triangles formed by three bulbs, there must be the maximum number of right triangles.

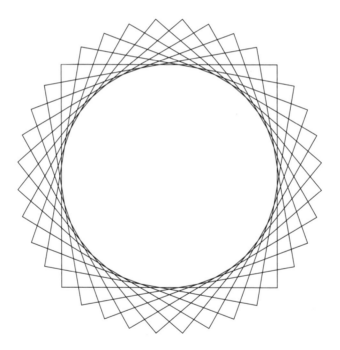

❖ State how many right triangles Daphne found, and draw a possible configuration.

21 ❖ Sea Figures

On the Sea of Ballerinas, next to the Dancing Sands, not far away from the Cape of Good Steps, a strange nautical ballet occured between three ships: the Victory *(V)*, the Willoughby *(W)*, and the Xylophone *(X)*, and three buoys: *A*, *B*, and *C*. *A*, *B*, and *C* are set as in the figure below.

The Victory leaves *B* at exactly the time when the Willoughby and the Xylophone leave *C*. The speed of all ships is absolutely constant.

The Victory is sailing toward *A* and reaches it after one hour. Both the Victory and the Willoughby move at the same speed, but the Willoughby is traveling on the straight line *AC*, going away from *A*.

As for the Xylophone, it travels in such a way that at all times the quadrilateral *BVWX* is a parallelogram.

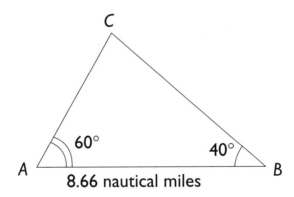

C

60° 40°

A
8.66 nautical miles
B

❖ What is the speed of the Xylophone in knots, rounded to the nearest hundredth?

You can use:

$\sqrt{2} \approx 1.414$, $\sqrt{3} \approx 1.732$, $\sqrt{5} \approx 2.236$
1 knot = 1 nautical mile per hour, 1 nautical mile = 1,852 meters

22 ❖ The Mirrors

Two identical rectangular mirrors are set vertically. They form an angle measuring 1 degree. The edges of the mirrors are x units apart on one side and $2x$ units apart on the other. The mirrors are shown from above in the figure, and the angles are not accurate.

A horizontal light beam hits one of the mirrors.

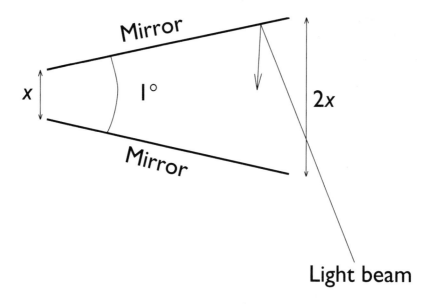

❖ What is the maximum number of reflections of the beam of light?

23 ❖ The Six Faces of the Pyramid

The pyramid below has six faces, whose areas form an arithmetic progression: S, $2S$, $3S$, $4S$, and $5S$ for the triangular faces, and $6S$ for the pentagonal base.

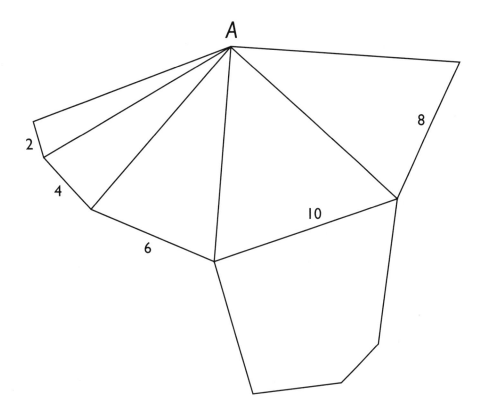

❖ What is the area of the smallest triangle? Round your answer to the nearest tenth.

CHAPTER 4

Arithmetic and Combinatorics

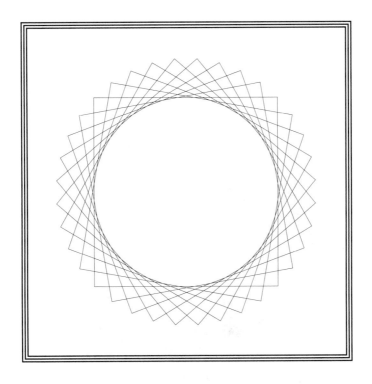

24 ❖ The Tournament

In a chess tournament, each competitor has played exactly one game with every other competitor. Five of them lost two games each. All the others won two games apiece.

There were no draws.

❖ How many competitors were there?

25 ❖ Sum One

If I work out this problem:

$$
\begin{array}{r}
1 \\
+\ 11 \\
+\ 111 \\
+\ 1111 \\
\cdots\cdots\cdots\cdots\cdots \\
+\ 1111111111111\ \cdots\cdots\cdots\ 111111111111
\end{array}
$$

(In the last line—the 96th—the digit 1 is repeated 96 times.)

????????? .... ??????????????????

❖ How many 1's will be in the result?

26 ❖ Consistent Numbers

Constance enjoys playing with numbers. Her favorite game is to take a number, work out the product of its digits, and do the same with the number she has obtained—until she ends up with a one-digit number.

$23 \rightarrow 2 \times 3 = 6$
$54 \rightarrow 5 \times 4 = 20 \rightarrow 2 \times 0 = 0$
$999 \rightarrow 9 \times 9 \times 9 = 729 \rightarrow 7 \times 2 \times 9 = 126 \rightarrow 1 \times 2 \times 6 = 12 \rightarrow 1 \times 2 = 2$

The *persistence* of a number is the number of multiplication steps necessary to get to a one-digit number. For example, the persistence of 6 is 0, the persistence of 23 is 1, for 54 it is 2, and for 999 it is 4. Constance is especially interested in the numbers whose persistence is greater than or equal to 4, and she calls them *consistent numbers.*

❖ What is the smallest consistent number?

27 ❖ Eurocking Chairs

In this border town, the shopkeepers indicate the prices in both francs and deutsche marks, and they give change in euros. This morning, at an antique shop, I found two beautiful chairs. To my surprise, the price in marks and the price in francs for the pair of chairs are two integers with the same four digits, only in a different order. Today the exchange rate was 10 francs for 3 marks and 2 marks for 1 euro.

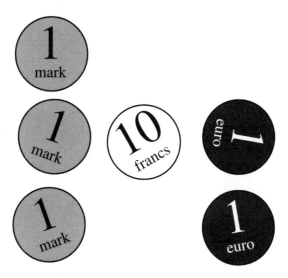

❖ If I pay for the chairs with 500-franc bills, how many euros will I get as change?

Note: The rate between francs, deutsche marks, and euros is now fixed.

28 ❖ The Remaining Cells

Four cogwheels roll on a tape printed with 1,995 identical square cells, numbered from 1 to 1,995.

The first cogwheel perforates one cell every four cells, starting with cell number 4.
The second cogwheel does the same, but every five cells, starting with the number 5.
The third perforates every seven cells, starting with the number 7.
The last perforates every thirteen cells, beginning with cell number 13.

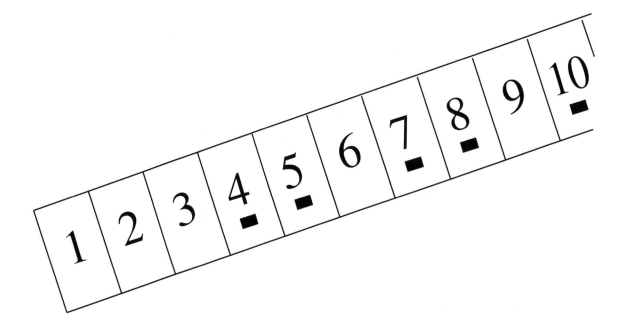

❖ When the four wheels have run through the whole tape, how many cells will remain intact?

29 ❖ Upside Down

The number 1995 can be read upside down as 5661, using the digits as they are shown here, whereas 1994 cannot, as the digit 4, like 3 and 7, can't be read upside down.

❖ Starting with 1, the fifth number that can be read upside down is 8, and the 15th is 21, but what is the 1995th?

30 ❖ Ring Fingers

Far, far away in space, on an unexplored planet, a close encounter of the fourth kind has occurred: Little blue men have met little green men. They are quite amazed to see that their hands do not have the same number of fingers: 7 for the blue and 8 for the green. Yet the scientists of both planets are quick to notice that, counting on the fingers as the figure shows, some numbers can be counted both on blue ring fingers and on green ring fingers!

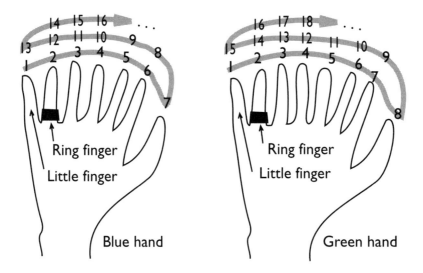

❖ How many such numbers are there between 1,896 and 1,996? Give two of them.

31 ❖ Drive-Through

F OCE can sometimes be a little bit clumsy. Today, while trying out his brand-new VOLVO, he decided to buy himself lunch.

Alas! One false move and his coffee spilled all over the leather seats!

$$\frac{\text{FOCE}}{\text{VOLVO}} = 0.\text{COFFEECOFFEE}\ldots$$

As in all cryptarithms, two different letters always stand for two different numbers and vice versa. Note that here the integral part of the quotient (that is, 0) is actually the number 0 and not the letter O.

❖ Find the value of COFFEE.

32 ❖ The Nine Factors

All the numbers from 1 to 9 were placed in the nine triangular cells shown in the drawing. A minus sign was added in front of some of the numbers.

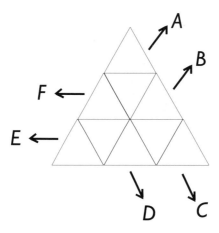

The letters *A*, *B*, *C*, *D*, *E*, and *F* are the products of three or five of those numbers.

A	*B*	*C*	*D*	*E*	*F*
320	162	6,048	−60	756	−240

❖ Find the right place in the triangle for each number.

50 Mathematical Puzzles and Problems ◆ *Red Collection*
©2001 Key Curriculum Press

33 ❖ Red Light/Green Light

Nina is observing the signals of two laser beams, *A* and *B*. These signals are periodic and so short that they can be considered instantaneous.

Nina observes that both signals are emitted exactly at time 0.

Laser *A* has a red signal. Not counting the first signal (at time 0), Nina sees 5 signals in 6 minutes.

Laser *B* has a green signal. Not counting the first one, Nina observes 32 signals in 31 minutes.

After one and a half hours of thorough observation, Nina has never seen two signals at exactly the same time. Yet she has noticed that some signals are really very close.

❖ What are the order numbers of the signals (counting the first ones as the 0th) that are the closest to each other during Nina's observation? How much time elapses between them?

34 ❖ Closing Up Fractions

Frank and Joe are playing the closest fraction game. They randomly choose a fraction; this time it is 225/157. Then the players take turns giving a fraction that abides by these three conditions:

- It is not equal to the original fraction.
- The difference between the numerator and the denominator is less than or equal to 1,995.
- It must be a better approximation of the original fraction than the fraction given by the opponent.

Being formidable numerical duelists, the opponents face off very excitedly until one of them throws in the final, winning fraction. That puts an end to the game!

❖ What is the last, closest fraction?

35 ❖ The Multidivisible Cube

The cube of a positive integer has five times as many divisors as the integer does itself.

❖ How many divisors does the square of the original number have?

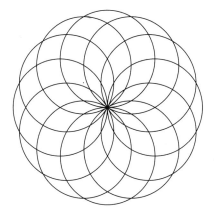

CHAPTER 5

Equations and Systems

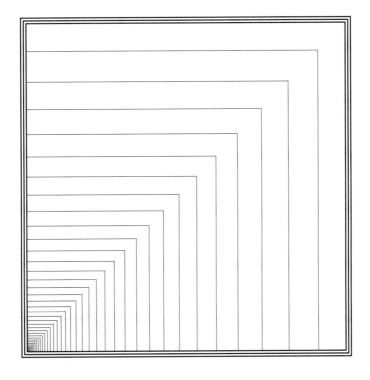

36 ❖ Logoniversary

On their wedding anniversary, Ada and Charles are playing on the computer. On the monitor is a grid on which an animal can be moved. At the beginning, the animal is situated in the top left cell, looking to the right. To move the animal, you must click on these two icons:

This one moves the animal forward.

This one makes the animal turn 90 degrees clockwise without advancing.

The sequence shown below left corresponds to the path shown below right.

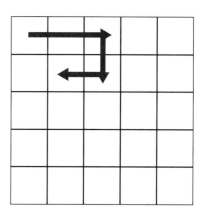

Beginning at the starting cell of a large grid, Charles intends to go through all the cells, ending at the last cell. His wife asks him, "Do you know that you will have to click a number of times equal to or more than the year of our wedding day?"

❖ In what year were Ada and Charles married?

37 ❖ Raymond's Pond

In Raymond's pond there are 128 amphibians, either tadpole or frog. As everybody knows, tadpoles have a tail, while frogs have lost theirs growing up. All frogs have four legs, while tadpoles, according to how old they are, can have four legs, two legs, or none (see drawing).

It took him quite a while, but Raymond was able to count 264 legs and 113 tails in his pond. While he was counting, he noticed that one kind of tadpole was twice as numerous as another.

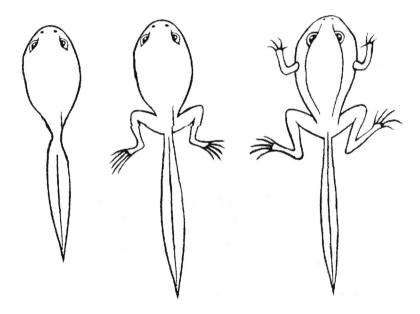

❖ How many two-legged tadpoles are there in Raymond's pond?

38 ❖ Statistics

The International Championship of Mathematics and Logic has entries in many categories, including HC (High Competitors), GP (General Public), and L1 (Undergraduate).

In a statistical study of 1,000 entries, all from the categories HC, GP, and L1, Allan, who has analyzed all the forms, informs Alex, who will compute all the data, that on question 14:

- Exactly 10% of the HC are wrong.
- Exactly 50% of the L1 are wrong.
- Exactly 40% of the GP are wrong.

Alex computes the number of wrong answers for question 14. Allan checks his result and comes to twice Alex's result before realizing that he had swapped the percentages of HC and GP and that Alex's result is correct.

❖ How many L1 entries were there?

39 ❖ The Five Numbers

The teacher wrote five numbers on the back of the blackboard. Then on the front of the board, he wrote the numbers 6, 7, 8, 8, 9, 9, 10, 10, 11, and 12. These numbers are the ten possible sums of two of the five hidden numbers.

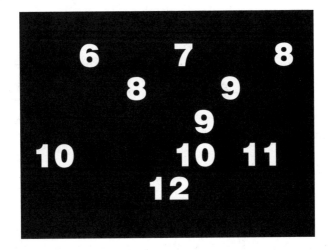

❖ What are the five hidden numbers? List the numbers in ascending order.

40 ❖ The Prophecy of Nostradaplus

At the beginning of the 13th century, Simon de Montfort asked the numerologist Nostradaplus to predict which would be the "major years." The sibylline answer was:

In the following years, as in the distant future, the major years will be those whose four decimal digits "abcd" satisfy the following condition:

$$\boxed{a \quad b} \; + \; \boxed{c \quad d} \; = \; \boxed{b \quad c}$$

It is interesting to note that in 1208, Simon de Montfort started his crusade against the inhabitants of Albi, and $12 + 08 = 20$.

❖ Can you be as clairvoyant as Nostradaplus and say how many four-digit major years there are? What are the next two major years after 1995?

41 ❖ Syldavian Exchanges

In Syldavia, the official currency is the Syldavian crown. But the inhabitants, who have been collectors since time immemorial, also use stamps, corks, and phone cards for their exchanges.

One Syldavian crown always equals x stamps, y corks, and z cards, the integers x, y, and z being consecutive, but not necessarily in that order.

You know that:

- 9 cards are worth one more Syldavian crown than 8 corks.
- 8 stamps are worth two more Syldavian crowns than 6 cards.
- 6 stamps are worth two more Syldavian crowns than 4 corks.

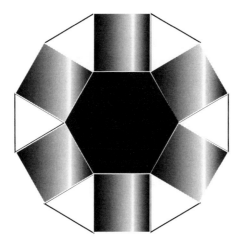

❖ If you exchange (at the official rate) one Syldavian crown for stamps, another one for corks, and a last one for cards, how many items do you have?

42 ❖ The Golf Ball

On a regulation golf ball, most of its 384 small dimples (arranged triangularly) are surrounded by 6 others, but a few dimples are surrounded by only 5 others.

❖ How many dimples are surrounded by only 5 others?

A Matter of Logic

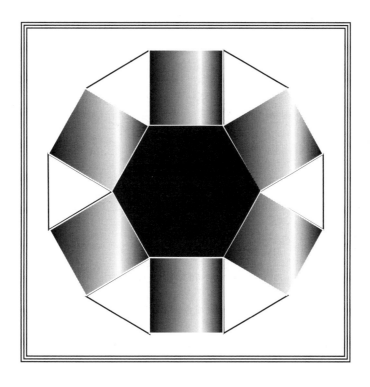

43 ❖ Memorization

Captain Memo has no memory! When he had to choose a code for his safe, he picked a number that he could remember easily.

His code is the smallest number such that, when you write the digit 1 in front of it (that is, on its left), and another 1 behind (that is, on its right), the number thus obtained equals 99 times the original code number.

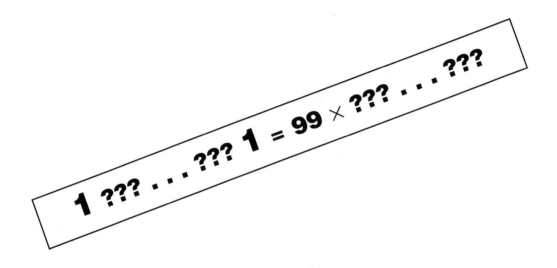

$$1 \, ??? \ldots ??? \, 1 = 99 \times ??? \ldots ???$$

❖ What is the sum of the digits of Captain Memo's code?

44 ❖ Stepping Stones

Matthew has four boxes forming a cross in front of him. The boxes contain a lot of stones (more than 50 in each box). He takes the stones from box *A* and puts them one by one into boxes *B, C, D, A, B,* and so on, until all have been distributed. He then throws away the contents of box *A*. After that, he takes the stones from box *B* and puts them one by one into boxes *C, D, A, B, C,* and so on, until all have been distributed. He then throws away the contents of box *B*. He continues the same process with boxes *C, D, A, B,* and so on. The game is over when, after having distributed all the remaining stones, he has none to throw away.

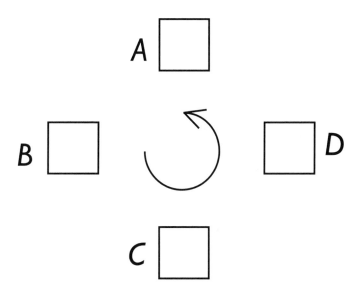

❖ How many stones are left when he stops playing?

45 ❖ Lucky's Race

Lucky Swift, the bicycle racer who starts faster than her own shadow, goes out for a ride.

She lives on Dalton Avenue, where the traffic lights are either red or green (never yellow) and are exactly 500 meters apart.

These lights are set in a very simple way: They all turn red at the same time (and stay red for 20 seconds), and then they turn green all at once (staying green for 30 seconds).

It takes Lucky 1 minute and 14 seconds to cover 500 meters, whether she is at first stationary or moving. She never runs a red light, but she is allowed to pass at the precise moment when the traffic lights change color.

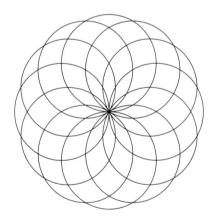

❖ What is the maximum number of lights Lucky can go through without stopping?

46 ❖ The Four Letters

Add four letters to the box below so that:

- The sentence written in the box is true.
- The four added letters, read vertically, make a word meaning something that can be thrown.

INSIDE THIS RECTANGLE

TWO	"..."S
THREE	"..."S
FOUR	"..."S
FIVE	"..."S

CAN BE SEEN

47❖Knossos

King Minos of Crete wishes to use a 60-meter–by–100-meter rectangle to build the Minotaur's labyrinth at his Palace of Knossos (see figure). The walls will be built to follow a grid of 10-meter squares, and they are bound by the intersections of that grid and the following conditions:

- Any cell can be reached from either the entrance or the exit.
- The entrance and the exit are connected.

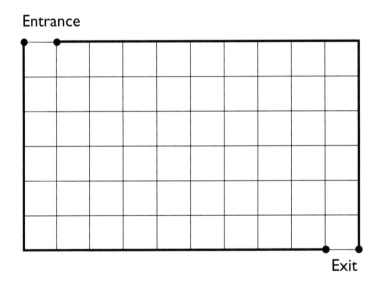

Entrance

Exit

❖ What is the maximum total length of the walls that can be built, in meters?

48 ❖ Traffic Lights

Frederick, who fancies himself a mathematician, uses his computer to simulate the traffic on a main street of his city. He assumes that on this street there are n traffic lights, numbered from 1 to n, and at any given moment, each light is either red, yellow, or green.

In order to optimize the traffic, Frederick says that there is one condition to fulfill: p and q being any different numbers, if traffic lights number p and number q have the same color, then traffic light number $p + q$ has another color.

❖ What is the maximum possible value of n?

49 ❖ Getting Even

You face your opponent Joe in a number game. There are 1,995 pawns on the table. Each player must take, in turns, 1, 2, 3, 4, or 5 pawns. The aim is to have an even number of pawns when all have been removed. You start the game.

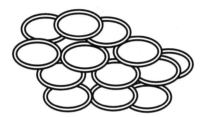

❖ Can you win? If so, how many pawns must you take on your first move so that you are certain to win, no matter how Joe plays?

Answer 0 if you think that Joe will win.

50 ❖ Scrooge's Ingots

Scrooge's ingots are nine right parallelepipeds: *A, B, C, D, E, F, G, H,* and *I.*
All have the same height and are made of the same material. Their bases are
nine squares, all different, and their sides measure, in centimeters, whole
numbers from 1 to 9.

With a pair of scales, Scrooge notes that:

- *A* is lighter than *D.*
- *B* is lighter than *C.*
- *D* is lighter than *G.*
- *E* is lighter than *F.*
- *H* is lighter than *I.*
- *A* + *B* + *C* weighs the same as *E* + *F* + *G.*
- *B* + *C* + *D* weighs the same as *G* + *H* + *I.*

❖ Give the respective lengths of the nine sides of the bases of Scrooge's ingots
  in centimeters.

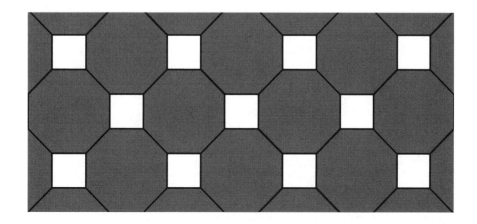

❖ SOLUTIONS ❖

1. The Shortcut

The usual course is $OA + OB = 57 + 43 = 100$ m.

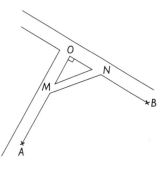

With $AM = MN = NB = x$ (in meters), the shortest course is $AM + MN + NB = 3x$.

The lengths of the two smallest sides of the triangle MNO, right-angled at O, are: $OM = OA - AM = 57 - x$, and $ON = OB - BN = 43 - x$. Using the Pythagorean Theorem, we get $OM^2 + ON^2 = MN^2$, or $(57 - x)^2 + (43 - x)^2 = x^2$, which leads to the equation $x^2 - 200x + 5{,}098 = 0$.

This equation has two possible solutions:
$x = 100 + \sqrt{4{,}902}$ and $x = 100 - \sqrt{4{,}902} \approx 29.99$

Since the shortcut is supposed to be shorter than the usual course of 100 m, only the second solution fits. The number of meters saved with the shortcut is $(OA + OB) - 3x \approx 100$ m $- 90$ m $= \textbf{10 m.}$

2. Doubloon Island

R must be one vertex. A second vertex, call it A, must lie on $\overline{TR}$. Call the third vertex B. The different possibilities for $\overline{RA}$, $\overline{RB}$, and $\overline{AB}$, in which two sides are 600 m and 400 m, are recorded in the table.

There are six possibilities, all shown on the next page. Notice that in two cases out of the six, two triangles can be constructed.

$\overline{RA}$	$\overline{RB}$	$\overline{AB}$
other length	600 m	400 m
400 m	600 m	other length
600 m	400 m	other length
other length	400 m	600 m
600 m	other length	400 m
400 m	other length	600 m

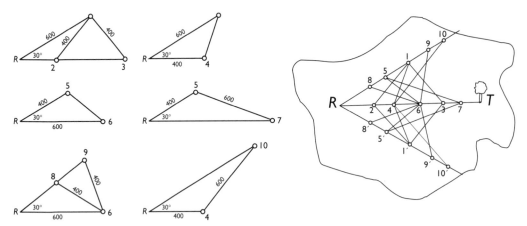

There are ten points, numbered from 1 to 10. Five of the points (2, 3, 4, 6, and 7) are on the line *TR,* and the other five have symmetric equivalents about $\overline{AB}$: $1'$, $5'$, $8'$, $9'$, and $10'$. So there are **15 possible sites** for the treasure.

3. Parallels

The figure shows the four possible parallelograms *A*, *B*, *C*, and *D*, that fit Mr. Tejada's conditions. *A* and *C* have the same area: $14 \times 7 = 98$ cm^2. In order to calculate the areas of *B* and *D*, first we need to know the respective lengths of their bases. Let *b* equal *B*'s base. Using the Pythagorean Theorem:

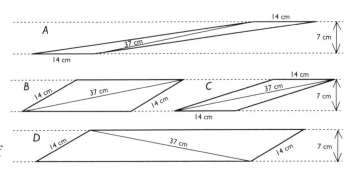

$$b = \sqrt{37^2 - 7^2} - \sqrt{14^2 - 7^2} = \sqrt{1,320} - \sqrt{147} = 2\sqrt{330} - 7\sqrt{3} \approx 24.2074486$$

Calculating the same for *d*:

$$d = \sqrt{37^2 - 7^2} - \sqrt{14^2 - 7^2} = \sqrt{1,320} - \sqrt{147} = 2\sqrt{330} - 7\sqrt{3} \approx 48.4561599$$

We see that *d* is approximately twice *b*'s value.
Let *x* be the diagonal's length. To make the equality $d = 2b$ true, we must have

$$\sqrt{x^2 - 7^2} + \sqrt{14^2 - 7^2} = 2\left(\sqrt{x^2 - 7^2} - \sqrt{14^2 - 7^2}\right), \text{ that is, } \sqrt{x^2 - 7^2} = 21\sqrt{3}.$$

Then $x = \mathbf{14\sqrt{7}}$ **cm** ≈ 37.04051835 cm.

4. Planet of the Games

First notice that the parallelogram can just as well be a rectangle, without changing any proportion of the regions. Linking each vertex to the middle of a side draws a parallelogram *EFGH;* its area is a fifth of the rectangle's (see figure).

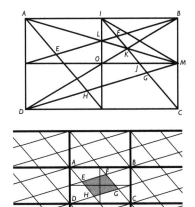

EFGH can be cut into four equal quadrilaterals by the perpendicular bisectors of *ABCD*'s sides. Each of them (for example, *OLFJ*) has an area equal to 1/20th of *ABCD*'s area.

$\overline{ML}$ and $\overline{OB}$ are the medians of triangle *IOM,* so their intersection point *K* is the circumcenter. There are six triangles that have *K* as one vertex, a vertex of *IOM* as another vertex, and a midpoint of a side of *IOM* as the third vertex. By a theorem of geometry, since *K* is the circumcenter of *IOM,* all six triangles have equal area, which is 1/6 the area of *IOM* or 1/12 the area of *IBOM,* or 1/48 the area of *ABCD.*

The area of *FKL* = area of *LFJO* − area of *OKJ* − area of *LKO*

$$= (1/20 - 1/48 - 1/48) \text{ area of } ABCD$$

$$= 1/120 \text{ area of } ABCD$$

So the number of people who like math games is 1/120th of the inhabitants of the planet—in other words, **100 people.**

5. Cake Walk

Let *TL* = *x*, *LM* = *y*, and *TM* = *z*. We have the equations $x + y = z + 1996$ and $x^2 + y^2 = z^2$.

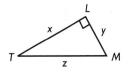

Pythagorean triples are of the form $x = k(m^2 - n^2)$, $y = 2kmn$, and $z = k(m^2 + n^2)$.

So $x + y - z = 1996$ leads, after substituting, simplifying, and factoring, to $2k(m - n) = 1996$, or $kn(m - n) = 998$.

So *k* and *n* must be divisors of 998: 1, 2, 499, or 998.

Solving $kn(m - n) = 998$ for *m* gives $m = (998/kn) + n$.

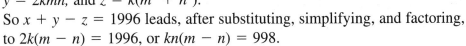

Here are all the possible combinations of values for k and n:

k	n	$m = \dfrac{998}{kn} + n$	$x = k(m^2 - n^2)$	$y = 2kmn$	$z = k(m^2 + n^2)$
1	1	999	998,000	1,998	998,002
1	2	501	250,997	2,004	251,005
1	499	501	2,000	499,998	500,002
1	998	999	1,997	1,994,004	1,994,005
2	1	500	499,998	2,000	500,002
(2)	(2)	(251.5)	(126,496.5)	(2,012)	(126,512.5)
2	499	500	1,998	998,000	998,002
499	**1**	**3**	**3,992**	**2,994**	**4,990**
499	**2**	**3**	**2,495**	**5,988**	**6,487**
998	**1**	**2**	**2,994**	**3,992**	**4,990**

In most of the cases, the total number of paces is more than 10,000 (and in the case $k = n = 2$, the number of paces is not an integer). Notice that the last line and the third-from-last line are really the same solution (for z), only with x and y interchanged.

So there are two possible solutions: The number of paces between Tania's house and Math's Chinese Bakery can be either **4,990** or **6,487.**

6. Polly and the Nonagon

Taking OA as a unit, we have
$OA = OB = AE = 1$. Triangle ABE is right-angled
at E, so $EB^2 = 2^2 - 1 = 3$, so $EB = \sqrt{3}$, and by
construction $FB = EB$.

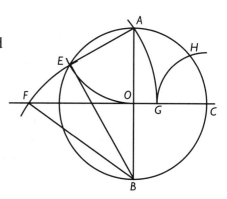

Calculate FO: Triangle FOB is right-angled
at O. So $FO^2 = FB^2 - OB^2 = \left(\sqrt{3}\right)^2 - 1 = 2$,
so $FO = \sqrt{2}$.

Calculate OG: $FG = FA = FB = \sqrt{3}$,
so $OG = FG - FO = \sqrt{3} - \sqrt{2}$.

Calculate CG: $CG = OC - OG =$
$1 - \left(\sqrt{3} - \sqrt{2}\right) = 1 - \sqrt{3} + \sqrt{2}$.

Using the data, $CG \approx 1 - 1.73205 + 1.41421 = 0.68216$.

Now calculate the true length of a side of a regular nonagon: $360°/9 = 40°$

The angle at the center equals $40°$, and half of that angle equals $20°$ (see figure).

We then have $L/2 = \sin 20°$, and $L = 2 \sin 20°$. Using the data, $L \approx 0.68404$.

So Polly Gone's polygon is not really regular.

Now calculate the size of the error as a percentage:

$(0.68216 - 0.68404)/0.68216 = -188/68{,}216 = -47/17{,}054 \approx -0.0027559 = -2.7559\%$.

Rounding to the nearest one-tenth of a percent, the error is **−0.3%.**

7. Mona and Lisa's Fields

Drawing the fields, we have: $b = ka$, $c = kb$, and $d = kc$, so $b = ka$, $c = k^2a$, and $d = k^3a$.

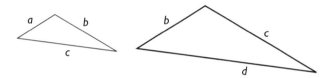

To have the smallest possible integers, we must have $k = 3/2$ and $a = 8$.

Then the sides of Mona's field are 8 hm, 12 hm, and 18 hm, and the sides of Lisa's field are 12 hm, 18 hm, and 27 hm.

The smallest possible perimeter is $8 + 12 + 18 =$ **38 hm.**

8. Gene's Swimming Pool

Let A, B, C, D, E, F, G, and H be the vertices of the pool, and let a, b, c, d, e, f, g, and h be the pool's sides. Because two consecutive sides must be perpendicular, a, c, e, and g are all parallel, while b, d, f, and h also are all parallel.

The location of B and C with respect to A is unique up to rotation and reflection. So for convenience, let's (arbitrarily) orient the drawing so that a is in the positive y-direction and b is in the positive x-direction.

Treating all sides as vectors, going around the pool we have $\vec{a} + \vec{b} + \vec{c} + \vec{d} + \vec{e} + \vec{f} + \vec{g} + \vec{h} = 0$. Projecting these vectors onto the x- and y-axes, we have (1) $a + c + e + g = 0$ and (2) $b + d + f + h = 0$.

In equation (1) we have $a = 10$ and $(c, e, g) = (\pm 30, \pm 50, \pm 70)$. The only possible solution is $10 - 30 - 50 + 70 = 0$, so $(c, e, g) = (-30, -50, +70)$. In equation (2) we have $b = 20$ and $(d, f, h) = (\pm 40, \pm 60, \pm 80)$. The only possible solution is $20 - 40 - 60 + 80 = 0$, so $(d, f, h) = (-40, -60, +80)$.

The solution appears in the figure. The pool is formed by three rectangles, whose areas can be found easily:

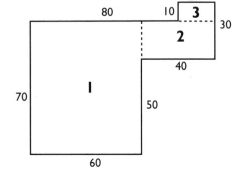

Rectangle 1: 60 m × 70 m = 4,200 m²
Rectangle 2: 40 m × 20 m =   800 m²
Rectangle 3: 10 m × 20 m =   200 m²

The area of Gene's pool is **5,200 m².**

9. The Discrete Theorem

The center of gravity of the triangle with vertices $A = (a_x, a_y, a_z)$, $B = (b_x, b_y, b_z)$, and $C = (c_x, c_y, c_z)$ is merely the point whose coordinates are the averages (means) of the coordinates of the vertices:

$$\left(\frac{a_x + b_x + c_x}{3}, \frac{a_y + b_y + c_y}{3}, \frac{a_z + b_z + c_z}{3} \right)$$

In order for the coordinates to be integers, we must have $a_x + b_x + c_x$ divisible by 3, and similarly for the other two coordinates. But notice that if $a_x + b_x + c_x$ is divisible by 3, then so is $(a_x \pm 3p) + (b_x \pm 3q) + (c_x \pm 3r)$. So if ABC is any triangle of the type we are looking for, then so is $A'B'C'$, whose coordinates are those of ABC plus or minus various multiples of 3. We can summarize that if ABC is a triangle of this type, then $a_x + b_x + c_x \equiv 0 \bmod 3$, and similarly for the y- and z-coordinates.

So we don't need to consider the *infinite* discrete 3-space, but only the *finite* discrete 3-space of integers mod 3, which has 27 points, ranging from $(0, 0, 0)$ to $(2, 2, 2)$, and whose name is $(\mathbf{Z}/3) \times (\mathbf{Z}/3) \times (\mathbf{Z}/3)$ or $(\mathbf{Z}/3)^3$.

The problem is now rephrased as, "What is n, the size of the smallest set of points from this space, such that we are guaranteed that the set contains three points, the sum of whose x-coordinates is congruent to 0 mod 3, and likewise for their y- and z-coordinates?"

But this size n is just one more than m, the size of the *largest* set of points from the space such that *no* three points from the set have the sum of their x-coordinates congruent to 0 mod 3, and likewise for their y- and z-coordinates.

Let's call any such set (whether the largest or not) a "good set." So now the problem is rephrased as, "What is (one more than) the size of the largest good set of points from $(\mathbf{Z}/3)^3$?"

We will solve the problem first in one dimension ("What is the size of the largest good set of points from the discrete 1-space of integers mod 3?"). This space is called $(\mathbf{Z}/3)^1$ or just $\mathbf{Z}/3$. Then we'll use that answer to solve the problem in two dimensions, then use *that* answer to solve the main problem. (Note that in one dimension we can't really talk about a "triangle," but that's okay, because we've replaced "triangle" with "set of three distinct points").

In 1-space the problem is trivial: The space $(\mathbf{Z}/3)^1$ only has three points, (0), (1), and (2). By inspection, the size of the largest possible good set is 2. The sets are $\{(0), (1)\}$, $\{(0), (2)\}$, and $\{(1), (2)\}$, since from $\{(0), (1), (2)\}$ we would be able to form $(0) + (1) + (2) = (3) \equiv 0$ mod 3.

Now for two dimensions: Assume we have a good set of points G from the discrete 2-space of integers mod 3, known as $(\mathbf{Z}/3)^2$. First let's partition the set G into three subsets: the set of those points whose x-coordinate is 0, which we'll call G_0, those whose x-coordinate is 1, called G_1, and those whose x-coordinate is 2, called G_2. (Each of these subsets may be empty.) For each $j = 0, 1, 2$, if $\vec{a}$, $\vec{b}$, and $\vec{c}$ are elements of G_j, then the x-coordinate of $\vec{a} + \vec{b} + \vec{c} = 3j \equiv 0$ mod 3. But since G is good, we can't have the y-coordinate of $\vec{a} + \vec{b} + \vec{c} \equiv 0$ mod 3, since then we would have $\vec{a} + \vec{b} + \vec{c} \equiv (0, 0)$ mod 3. This shows that if we define $p(G_j) = \{(a_y) \,|\, \vec{a} \in G_j\}$, the projection of G_j onto the y-axis, then each $p(G_j)$ is also good. Hence, each $p(G_j)$, and therefore each G_j, can only be as large as the maximal good set in 1-space. So already we have an upper bound on the answer for 2-space: We can't have more than $3 \cdot 2 = 6$ elements.

But it may not be possible to make each G_j the maximal size and still have G be good, so we need to analyze the situation in more detail. We will find a way to construct good sets in 2-space based on the ones we have found in 1-space. First we will pick no more than two points (including possibly none at all) from any one of the good sets we found for 1-space and put them in $p(G_0)$. We will do the same for $p(G_1)$, and we can pick from the same good set or a different one—it doesn't matter. Then we will see if our choices so far eliminate any of the points of 1-space from consideration (see the explanation in a couple of paragraphs), and pick no more than two of the remaining ones to put in $p(G_2)$. We will try to pick in such a way as to make $p(G_0)$ and $p(G_1)$, and hence G_0 and G_1, as large as possible, while eliminating as few as possible from consideration for inclusion in $p(G_2)$, thus also keeping G_2 as large as possible.

Let's start with the largest possible number of points in each of $p(G_0)$ and $p(G_1)$—two points in each.

Note: If $(a_y) \in p(G_0)$, that is, $\vec{a} = (0, a_y) \in G_0$, and $(b_y) \in p(G_1)$, that is, $\vec{b} = (0, b_y) \in G_1$, then we can't have $(c) = (-a_y - b_y) \in p(G_2)$, that is, $\vec{c} = (2, -a_y - b_y) \in G_2$ (where negation is mod 3: $-0 = 0$, $-1 = 2$, and $-2 = 1$), because then we would have

$$\vec{a} + \vec{b} + \vec{c} = (0 + 1 + 2, a_y + b_y - a_y - b_y) = (3, 0) \equiv (0, 0) \bmod 3$$

So we need to eliminate from consideration for $p(G_2)$ all points of the form $-a_y - b_y = -(a_y + b_y)$, where $(a_y) \in p(G_0)$ and $(b_y) \in p(G_1)$. Since we want to eliminate as few possibilities as we can, there should be as few *distinct* points of the form $(a_y + b_y)$ as possible. Noticing that $a_y + b_y = b_y - (-a_y)$, which is the same as a vector from (a_y) to (b_y), and taking $-p(G_0) = \{(-a_y) | (a_y) \in p(G_0)\}$, the set of *opposites* of $p(G_0)$, we see that now we want to minimize the number of vectors from $-p(G_0)$ to $p(G_1)$. This will be minimal if every member of $p(G_1)$ is the same as a member of $-p(G_0)$, that is, $p(G_1)$ is just the set of opposites of $p(G_0)$.

So if we want to have two points each in $p(G_0)$ and $p(G_1)$, what we must do is pick any two points for $p(G_0)$, pick the opposites of those points for $p(G_1)$—for example, the opposite of $(0, 2)$ is $(0, 1)$—then find all possible sums of a member of $p(G_0)$ and a member of $p(G_1)$, and eliminate the opposites of those sums for consideration in $p(G_2)$.

Here's an example of the process:

Let $p(G_0) = \{(0), (1)\}$ and $p(G_1) = \{(0), (2)\}$. Then the possible sums are $(0) + (0) = (0)$, $(0) + (2) = (2)$, $(1) + (0) = (0)$, and $(1) + (2) = (0)$, or (0), (1), and (2). The opposites are $-(0) = (0)$, $-(1) = (2)$, and $-(2) = (1)$. This eliminates all possible points, so $p(G_2)$ is empty. Thus $G_0 = \{(0, 0), (0, 1)\}$, $G_1 = \{(1, 0), (1, 2)\}$, and G_2 is empty, so $G = \{(0, 0), (0, 1), (1, 0), (1, 2)\}$. By inspection, this is a good set—it's impossible to add three of these points to get $(0, 0) \bmod 3$.

Going back to our analysis, we discover by inspection that no matter how the points of $p(G_0)$ and $p(G_1)$ are chosen, there are *always* three distinct sums (with three distinct opposites). Since there are only three points in $(\mathbf{Z}/3)^1$, they all get eliminated, and $p(G_2)$ turns out to be empty, therefore, so does G_2. So in this case, the maximal size of a good set is 2 in G_0 plus 2 in G_1 plus 0 in $G_2 = 4$.

We must also examine the cases where G_0 or G_1 are smaller than 4—to see if that lets us get more points into G_2.

If one of G_0 has two points and the other only has one, then there are two distinct sums, so their two distinct opposites get eliminated from the three points in 1-space, leaving only one point for G_2, so the maximum is $1 + 2 + 1 = 4$.

If both G_0 and G_1 have one point, there is one sum, so one point gets eliminated, leaving two. So the maximum is $1 + 1 + 2 = 4$.

If either G_0 or G_1 has no points, then there is no sum, so no points get eliminated, leaving all three available. So the maximum is $0 + 1 + 2 = 3$ (or $0 + 0 + 2 = 2$).

So our answer for two dimensions is that the maximum size of a good set in $(\mathbf{Z}/3)^2$ is 4.

Whew! Now for the three-dimensional case—finally the answer we're looking for:

A similar argument shows that if G is a good set of points in $(\mathbf{Z}/3)^3$, then each $p(G_j) = \{(a_y, a_z) \mid (j, a_y, a_z) \in G\}$, the projection onto the yz-plane of those points in G whose first coordinate is j, is also good. (Here we must show that if the first coordinates of three points are the same, then we cannot have *both* the y-coordinates *and* the z-coordinates summing to 0 mod 3.) Hence, each of G_0, G_1, and G_2 can be no larger than the largest good set in $(\mathbf{Z}/3)^2$, which we just found to be 4. So an upper bound on the largest good set in $(\mathbf{Z}/3)^3$ is $3 \cdot 4 = 12$.

But again, it may not be possible to get a set that large. Again, a similar argument shows that $p(G_2)$ cannot contain any point of the form $(-a_y - b_y, -a_z - b_z)$ where $\vec{a} \in G_0$ and $\vec{b} \in G_1$, so again our method of construction is to pick no more than four (this time) elements from the good sets from $(\mathbf{Z}/3)^2$ to use for each of $p(G_0)$ and $p(G_1)$, eliminate all the opposites of the sums of one element from $p(G_0)$ and one element from $p(G_1)$, and from the points which haven't been eliminated, pick no more than four for $p(G_2)$.

Here is an example:

From the two-dimensional good set we found above, let's pick just one point (to keep the example small) for $p(G_0)$, namely $(1, 0)$, and two for $p(G_1)$, namely $(0, 0)$ and $(1, 2)$. Then the distinct sums are $(1, 0)$ and $(2, 2)$, so the distinct opposites are $(2, 0)$ and $(1, 1)$. Thus any 2-vector from $(\mathbf{Z}/3)^2$ is eligible except these two. Since $(\mathbf{Z}/3)^2$ contains $3^2 = 9$ points, this leaves seven to choose from. But we can only choose four. So we arbitrarily choose four of the remaining seven and put them in $p(G_2)$, which now gives us G_0, G_1, and G_2, which in turn gives us G.

Back to the analysis: If we want four points in $p(G_0)$ and four in $p(G_1)$, then a similar argument shows that the minimum number of points will be eliminated for $p(G_2)$ if $p(G_1)$ is the set of opposites of points in $p(G_0)$, and the number eliminated will be eight, leaving only one point eligible for $p(G_2)$. So the maximum is $4 + 4 + 1 = 9$.

If, for instance, we want $p(G_0)$ to have four elements and $p(G_1)$ to have three elements, then again, by making those three points the opposites of three of the points in $p(G_0)$, the minimum number of points, namely seven, will be eliminated, leaving two, so the maximum is $4 + 3 + 2 = 9$.

If we want each of $p(G_0)$ and $p(G_1)$ to have three points, then making $p(G_1)$ the opposite of $p(G_0)$ achieves the minimum elimination—six points—leaving three, so the maximum is $3 + 3 + 3 = 9$.

In all smaller cases of $p(G_0)$ and $p(G_1)$, we can show that at most five points need to be eliminated, always leaving at least four to choose from, so the maximum is less than or equal to $3 + 2 + 4 = 9$.

Thus the maximum size of a good set in $(\mathbf{Z}/3)^3$ is 9.

So our final answer is that you need at least **10 points** in discrete 3-space (no longer just mod 3) to be sure that at least one triangle has a center of gravity with integer coefficients.

---

10. Five with One Blow

At first, let's ignore the condition of turning 5 dials together.

In that case, to get all the white parts facing down would take at least $32 \times 2 = 64$ thirds of a turn. And if we happened to turn one of the dials more than 2/3 of a turn, we would be obliged to finish the turn that we started. It would then take at least $64 + 3k$ thirds of a turn.

Now let's consider turning 5 dials together. That condition means that the total number of steps (expressed in thirds of a turn) is a multiple of 5. And the smallest number of the form $64 + 3k$ that is a multiple of 5 is 70—that is, 14 steps.

The diagram shows that it is possible to turn 31 dials out of the 32 by 2 thirds, while the remaining dial turns 2 thirds + 2 entire turns (that is, 8 thirds).

The minimum number of steps is actually **14.**

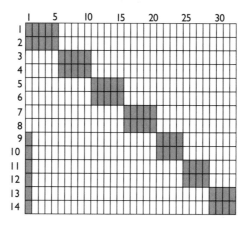

11. A Little Bit of Cutting Up

The illustration shows how to cut the figure up into four parts of exactly the same size and shape.

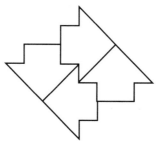

12. Soaking It Up

First, let's note that C, the center of diameter $\overline{AB}$, will move on a quarter-circle with center O and radius 10 cm. This is because triangle AOB is right-angled at O, its hypotenuse $\overline{AB}$ has a constant length of 20 cm, and $\overline{OC}$ is the median of $\overline{AB}$.

Let L be any point on the sponge. According to the Triangle Inequality,
$OL \le OC + CL$.

Now $OC = 10$ and $OL \le 10$, so $OL \le 20$. Any point L on the sponge will always be in or on the quadrant of center O and radius 20 cm.

In the same way, it can be proved that for any point M on or in that quadrant, there is a way the sponge can be placed so that it covers that point M.

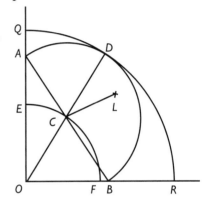

If $OM \le 10$, then M is either in the semi-circle $(E, 10$ cm$)$, that is, the initial position of the sponge, or in the semi-circle $(F, 10$ cm$)$, that is, the final position of the sponge.

If $10 \le OM \le 20$, then M is in the semi-circle $(C, 10$ cm$)$, C being the intersection of OM with the arc EF.

The washed area will then be the area of the quadrant: $\pi r^2/4 = \pi \cdot 20^2/4 = 100\pi$

Using $\pi = 3.14$, the area equals **314 cm²**.

13. Net Volume

To have the edges meet properly, we must have

$$AD_1 = AD_2 = D_1C = CD_3 = 15$$

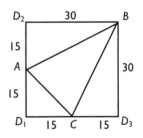

A, B, and C are the three vertices of the tetrahedron, and D_1, D_2 and D_3 glued together make the fourth vertex.

Since the net is a square, $\overline{BD}$ is perpendicular to $\overline{AD}$ and to $\overline{CD}$; therefore, it is perpendicular to the plane of the side ACD. Then ACD can be the base of the tetrahedron, and $\overline{BD}$ is its altitude.

The volume of $ABCD$ = area of $ACD \times BD/3 = (15 \times 15/2) \times 30/3 = 225 \times 30/6 = 1{,}125$ cm³.

The volume of the box was **1,125 cm³**.

14. Sweet Tetrahedron

There are two possibilities: The two sides of the cube where there is no vertex of the tetrahedron are either opposite or adjacent.

If the sides are opposite (Figure 2), the tetrahedron is not a real one, since the four vertices are coplanar.

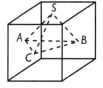

Figure 1

So the sides have to be adjacent (Figure 1).

The volume of a pyramid is $V = 1/3(bh)$, where b is the area of the base and h the altitude.

Let x be the edge of the cube. If ABC is the base, then $h = x/2$ and $b = x^2/4$. The volume is then $V = x^3/24$.

If $V = 9$ cm^3, then $x^3 = 216 = 6^3$.

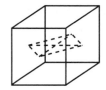

Figure 2

So the volume of sugar removed was $216 - 9 =$ **207 cm^3.**

15. A Crystal Ball?

Each disk can be inscribed in a square. Thus the solid can be placed in the interior of a cube (Figure 1). Let's take one of the disks. Since the shadow projected is the disk, the solid fits in the interior of a cylinder with that disk as the base (Figure 2). The same is true for the other disks. The solid is therefore included in each of three perpendicular cylinders. To have the maximum volume, the solid must be the intersection of the three cylinders.

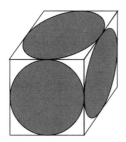

Figure 1

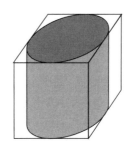

Figure 2

Let's begin by determining the intersection of two cylinders. They have the same diameter and are concurrent and orthogonal. The intersection of the two external envelopes of the cylinders consists of two ellipses obtained by cutting the cylinders at a 45° angle. The ellipses cut each other in the centers of two faces of the initial cube. The faces of the solid obtained are four sections of cylinders bounded by the ellipses described above (Figure 3).

The intersection of the two cylinders with the third will cause four other ellipses to appear, intersecting each other in pairs in the centers of the faces of the cube, and three at a time at the vertices of the cube (Figure 4).

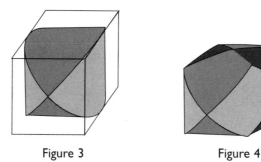

Figure 3   Figure 4

So the solid is comprised of **12 faces** bordered by 24 edges and meeting at 14 vertices.

16. The Angle-Scraping Machine

First let's notice that as the small rods are all equal, *AEBI, BFCJ,* and *CGDK* are all rhombuses, and their opposite angles are equal.

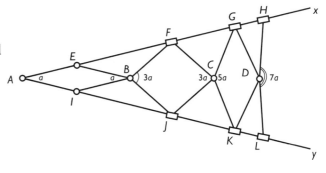

Second, for the same reason, the triangles *EBF, FCG, GDH, IBJ, JCK,* and *KDL* are all isosceles, and the angles of their bases are equal.

Let a be the measure of $\angle xAy$.

$$\angle EBI = \angle BEF = \angle BFE = \angle BIJ = \angle BJI = a$$
$$\angle JBF = \angle JCF = 360° - a - 2 \cdot (180° - 2a) = 3a$$
$$\angle BFC = \angle BJC = (360° - 2 \cdot 3a)/2 = 180° - 3a$$
$$\angle CFG = \angle CJK = \angle CGF = \angle CKJ = 180° - a - (180° - 3a) = 2a$$
$$\angle GCK = \angle GDK = 360° - 3a - 2 \cdot (180° - 4a) = 5a$$
$$\angle CGD = \angle CKD = (360° - 2 \cdot 5a)/2 = 180° - 5a$$
$$\angle DGH = \angle DHG = \angle DKL = \angle DLK = 180° - 2a - (180° - 5a) = 3a$$
$$\angle HDL = 360° - 5a - 2 \cdot (180° - 2 \cdot 3a) = 7a$$

If the desired angle at D is $112°$, then $\angle A$ is $112°/7 = 16°$, and the desired angle at B is $3 \times 16 = \textbf{48°}$.

Note: A figure representing this apparatus can be found in a posthumous work of the Marquis de l'Hôpital, "Traité analytique des sections coniques et de leur usage pour la resolution des equations dans les problèmes tant déterminez qu'indéterminez," 1720 ("Analytic Treatise of Conic Sections and of Their Use in Solving Definite and Indefinite Equations").

17. The Legacy of Circulus

To maximize the desired radius, we suppose that the figure is rotationally symmetrical for rotations around the center O (center of gravity of the triangle) by angles that are multiples of $120°$.

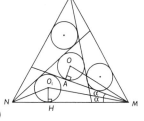

Letting $\triangle OAM$ be right-angled at A, we can write

$$r = OA = 8 \cdot \frac{2}{3} \cdot \frac{\sqrt{3}}{2} \sin(30° - 2\alpha) = \frac{8\sqrt{3}}{3} \sin(30° - 2\alpha)$$

Considering the two right triangles $\triangle NO_1H$ and $\triangle MO_1H$, we can write $r[\cot(30° - \alpha) + \cot \alpha] = 8$, from which we get $r = 8\cos(30° - 2\alpha) - 4\sqrt{3}$. The identity $\sin^2 x + \cos^2 x = 1$, for $x = 30° - 2\alpha$, gives

$$\left(\frac{\sqrt{3}}{8}\right)^2 r^2 + \left(\frac{r + 4\sqrt{3}}{8}\right)^2 = 1$$

So $3r^2 + \left(r^2 + 48 + 8r\sqrt{3}\right) = 64$, or $4r^2 + 8r\sqrt{3} - 16 = 0$.

The positive solution (in km) of this equation is $r = \sqrt{7} - \sqrt{3}$. Taking 2.646 for $\sqrt{7}$ and 1.732 for $\sqrt{3}$, we get 0.914 km or **914 meters.**

18. Sinuous

Let's calculate the first values of 2^n, the values of 2^n modulo 360, and the sizes of the acute angles (between $-90°$ and $+90°$) that have the same sine as the values in the second column. We notice that there is a periodicity. Starting with $n = 15$ we have $\sin 2^n = \sin 2^{n-12}$. Examining the values in one period shows that the greatest sine that can be obtained is $\sin 64°$. The first time this happens is for $\textbf{n = 6.}$

2^n	mod 360	Acute angle	2^n	mod 360	Acute angle
$2^0 = 1$	1	1	$2^{10} = 1,024$	304	-56
$2^1 = 2$	2	2	$2^{11} = 2,048$	248	-68
$2^2 = 4$	4	4	$2^{12} = 4,096$	136	44
$2^3 = 8$	8	8	$2^{13} = 8,192$	272	-88
$2^4 = 16$	16	16	$2^{14} = 16,364$	184	-4
$2^5 = 32$	32	32	$2^{15} = 32,768$	8	8
$2^6 = 64$	64	64	$2^{16} = 65,536$	16	16
$2^7 = 128$	128	52	$2^{17} = 131,072$	32	32
$2^8 = 256$	256	-76	$2^{18} = 262,144$	64	64
$2^9 = 512$	152	28	$2^{19} = 524,288$	128	52

19. Mathematica's Jewels

First let's study the properties of such a triangle to figure out how to construct it (see Figure 1).

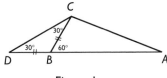

Figure 1

Assume ABC is such a triangle, and that $\overrightarrow{AB}$ has been extended to D so that $BD = BC$. By a theorem of geometry, $\angle BDC + \angle BCD = \angle ABC = 60°$. Since $\triangle BDC$ is isosceles, $\angle BDC = \angle BCD = 30°$. So we can construct two such triangles on the map as follows (see Figure 2 on the next page).

On the Boardwalk, draw $AD = AC + BC = 11$ km. From D draw $\overline{DE}$, making $\angle BDE = 30°$. Draw an arc with center A and radius $AC = 7$ km, intersecting $\overline{DE}$ at C_1 and C_2. From C_1 draw a line at an angle of $30°$ to $\overline{DE}$, intersecting $\overline{AD}$ at B_1, and similarly from C_2 to B_2.

We now have two triangles, AB_1C_1 and AB_2C_2, which you can show to be congruent. Now create two more placements of the triangle by rotating $\triangle AB_1C_1$ so that $\overline{AC_1}$ is on $\overline{AD}$, once with A of the triangle placed at the original point A and once with C_1 of the triangle placed at the original point A.

Finally, draw the reflections of all four triangles across the line perpendicular to $\overline{AD}$ at A (see Figure 3).

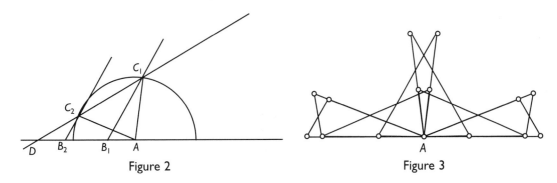

Figure 2   Figure 3

In total there are fifteen points, A included. There were **15 jewels.**

20. Daphne's Daffodils

Let's first notice that six points, with no three in line, determine

$_6C_3 = (6 \times 5 \times 4)/(3 \times 2 \times 1) = 20$ triangles.

Also, the condition that three points must never be in line implies that the number of right-angled triangles equals the number of right angles (one right angle cannot belong to two different triangles).

Let A be one of the six points. Let's suppose that two of the points, B and C, form with A a right angle A_1. A third point alone cannot form a right angle adjacent to A_1 (since three points must not be in line). So it takes two other points, D and E, to form a second right angle at A. The fifth and last point cannot form another right angle, always for the same reason. So the point A can be the vertex of only two right angles.

The same goes for all six points. So at the most, there can be only $2 \times 6 = 12$ right angles—that is, **12 right triangles.** Such combinations do exist, as shown by the two examples in the figure. Among the possibilities is the regular hexagon.

In fact, each and every hexagon whose vertices are determined by the extremities of three distinct diameters of the same circle is also a possible solution, since each hexagon contains three different rectangles.

21. Sea Figures

The figure shows the situation at an arbitrary time.

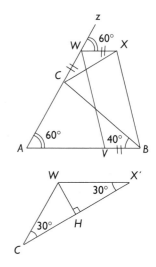

Draw $\overline{CX}$. Triangle CXW is isosceles because $CW = WX$ (V's and W's speeds are equal). $\angle XWz = \angle A = 60°$, and it is the exterior angle of triangle CXW, so $\angle XWz = \angle WCX + \angle WXC$.

Since $\angle WCX = \angle WXC$ (isosceles), $\angle WCX = 30°$. Notice that this means the direction of X is constant. When V arrives at A, after an hour, X has traveled a distance $H = CX'$ (see the figure below right). With $CW = AB = 8.66$ nautical miles, we have $\cos 30° = CH/CW = CH/AB$. Then $CH = AB \cos 30°$ and $CX' = 2AB \cos 30°$.

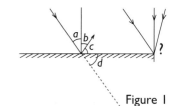

So $CX' = 8.66 \times \sqrt{3} \approx 8.66 \times 1.732 = 14.99912$, which can be rounded off to 15. The speed of the Xylophone is **15 knots.**

22. The Mirrors

Let's remember the rule of reflection: The angle of incidence ($\angle a$) is equal to the angle of reflection ($\angle b$) (see Figure 1). Also, $\angle c = \angle d$, which means that the reflected ray propagates along a trajectory symmetrical to the path it would take if it went *through* the mirror, rather than reflecting off it.

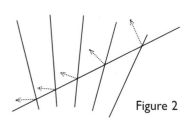

Figure 1

Note that the reflection does not occur off the surface of the glass, but off the ideally thin boundary between the glass and the silver at the back of the glass. Thus in the figures and the analysis, we can ignore the thickness of the glass, except for any refraction (bending of the light rays) that it might cause. To simplify the problem, we will ignore refraction.

Figure 2

This means that rather than considering reflections off of two mirrors, we may consider a straight line path through numerous mirrors, all at 1° to each other, as shown in Figures 2 and 3 (angles not drawn to scale). Figure 2 shows how successive reflections are equivalent to a straight line traversal.

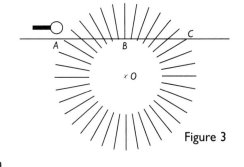

Figure 3

Figure 3 shows how the entire reflected path is equivalent to a single straight line traversal from *A* to *C*, except for some small details that we discuss below.

The fact that the distance between the lines in Figure 3 is $2x$ at the outside edges and x at the edges toward the center of the circle leads to the conclusion that $\angle AOC = 120°$. Let's study closely what happens at *A, B,* and *C* (Figure 4).

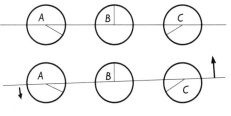

Figure 4

In all three cases, the beam touches the mirrors exactly on the edge, which means that there will be no reflection.

Even the slightest change in the trajectory would cause the trajectory to miss one of the three points. On the other hand, a different, very slight change of trajectory ensures a reflection at two out of the three points (Figure 4, bottom).

So the maximum number of reflections is **120.**

23. The Six Faces of the Pyramid

Since the areas and the bases of the five triangles form the same arithmetic progression, we conclude that the altitudes of the triangles must be equal. This means that the feet of the altitudes on the bases are equidistant from *T,* the common vertex. This is true whether the faces are cut open and lying flat, or folded up and joined to make the pyramid—the feet of the altitudes are *always* equidistant from *T,* and therefore *always* lie on a circle that is inscribed in the polygon formed by the bases of the triangles. In particular, this circle is inscribed in the pentagon that forms the base of the pyramid, and its center is *O* in the figure.

We have:

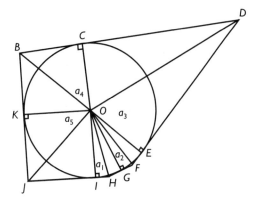

$HG = HI$
$IJ = JK = 4 - HI = 4 - HG$
$KB = BC = 6 - (4 - HG) = 2 + HG$
$CD = DE = 10 - (2 + HG) = 8 - HG$
$EF = GF = 8 - (8 - HG) = HG$

So $HG = HI = EF = GF = 1$,
$IJ = JK = BK = BC = 3$,
and $DC = DE = 7$.

Letting a_1 be half of $\angle IOG$ and letting R be
the radius of the inscribed circle, we get: $\tan a_1 = 3/R$, $\tan a_2 = 3/R$, $\tan a_3 = 3/R$,
$\tan a_4 = 3/R$, and $\tan a_5 = 3/R$. Using the formula

$$\tan(a + b) = \frac{\tan a + \tan b}{1 - \tan a \tan b}$$

we get, after much substitution and simplification,

$$\tan(a_1 + a_2 + a_3 + a_4 + a_5) = \frac{15R^4 - 178R^2 + 63}{R(R^4 - 78R^2 + 177)}$$

We know that $a_1 + a_2 + a_3 + a_4 + a_5 = 180°$ and $\tan 180° = 0$, so
$15R^4 - 178R^2 + 63 = 0$. Solving the equation leads to $R^2 = 11.5014968 \ldots$ or
$0.3651699 \ldots$, so $R = 3.391385 \ldots$ or $0.6042928 \ldots$.

It's clear from the geometry that R must be greater than 3, so the second solution
is extraneous. The area of the pentagon is $(R/2)(2 + 4 + 6 + 8 + 10) = 15R$,
and the area of the smallest triangle is 1/6 of the pentagon's area, namely
$15R/6 = 5R/2 = 2.5 \times 3.391385 = 8.479625 \approx 8.5$.

The area of the smallest triangle is **8.5**.

24. The Tournament

Let n be the number of competitors.

Each of the five players mentioned plays $n - 1$ games, losing 2 games, and winning
$(n - 1) - 2 = n - 3$ games. Each of the $n - 5$ other players also plays $n - 1$
games, winning 2 games, and losing $(n - 1) - 2 = n - 3$ games. So the number
of games lost is $5 \cdot 2 + (n - 5)(n - 3)$, and the number of games won is
$(n - 5) \cdot 2 + 5(n - 3)$.

50 Mathematical Puzzles and Problems ♦ *Red Collection*
©2001 Key Curriculum Press

Since they are equal (there were as many games lost as won), we get the equation

$$5 \cdot 2 + (n - 5)(n - 3) = 2(n - 5) + 5(n - 3)$$
$$n^2 - 15n + 50 = 0$$
$$(n - 5)(n - 10) = 0$$
$$n = 5 \text{ or } n = 10$$

- If $n = 5$, there were 5 competitors, each of them having lost 2 games and won 2. But then the number of remaining players is zero, which contradicts the statement that there *were* other players.
- If $n = 10$, there were 10 competitors. Five of them have lost 2 games and won 7, the five others having won 2 and lost 7. Each of the 10 played 9 others, so there were $(10 \cdot 9)/2 = 45$ games in total. (We divide by 2 so that each game is counted only once.)

	1	2	3	4	5	6	7	8	9	10
1		x	x	o	o	o	o	o	o	o
2	o		x	x	o	o	o	o	o	o
3	o	o		x	x	o	o	o	o	o
4	x	o	o		x	o	o	o	o	o
5	x	x	o	o		o	o	o	o	o
6	x	x	x	x	x		o	o	x	x
7	x	x	x	x	x	x		o	o	x
8	x	x	x	x	x	x	x		o	o
9	x	x	x	x	x	o	x	x		o
10	x	x	x	x	x	o	o	x	x	

The table shows that this is possible.

So there were **10 competitors.**

25. Sum One

First method:

Adding from right to left, we obtain:

123456790 123456790 . . . 123456790 123456790 123446

The period 123456790 repeats 10 times before the six digits 123446.

So the digit 1 appears **11 times** in that result.

Second method:

Let's study the general case: Let n be the number of digits on the last line, and S_n be the sum. We have: $S_n = n \cdot 1 + (n - 1) \cdot 10 + (n - 2) \cdot 10^2 + \ldots + 2 \cdot 10^{n-2} + 10^{n-1}$.

$$S_n = n\frac{10^n - 1}{9} - \sum_{k = 0}^{n - 1}(k \cdot 10^k)$$

By writing $f(x) = \sum_{k=0}^{n-1} x^k = \dfrac{x^n - 1}{x - 1}$ and taking the derivative of both sides with respect to x, then multiplying both sides by x, we get:

$$xf'(x) = \sum_{k=0}^{n-1} kx^k = x \cdot \frac{(n-1)x^n - nx^{n-1} + 1}{(x-1)^2}$$

So, $S_n = n\dfrac{10^n - 1}{9} - 10 \cdot \dfrac{(n-1)10^n - n \cdot 10^{n-1} + 1}{81} = \dfrac{10^{n+1} - 9n - 10}{81}$

For $n = 96$, that formula gives the following result:

$$S = \frac{10^{97} - 9 \cdot 96 - 10}{81} = \frac{10^{97} - 874}{81}$$

Carrying this out by hand, we find a period 123456790. That period repeats itself 10 times and is followed by 123446. So the digit 1 appears $10 + 1 = $ **11 times.**

26. Consistent Numbers

One-digit numbers all have a persistence that is zero. Let's see what happens with two-digit numbers. To do so, draw up a table of the products (just an ordinary multiplication table).

In the table, all the one-digit numbers, in ordinary type, are images of two-digit numbers whose persistence is 1 (10, 20, 30, . . . , 90, 11, 12, 21, 13, 31, . . . , 19, 91, 22, 23, 32, 24, 42, 33).
The two-digit numbers in bold type have a number of persistence 1 for their image, so they are themselves of persistence 2.

The numbers in bold, italic type have a number of persistence 2 for their image, so they are themselves of persistence 3.

Only one number remains in the table: 49, the image of 77.

	0	1	2	3	4	5	6	7	8	9
0	0	0	0	0	0	0	0	0	0	0
1	0	1	2	3	4	5	6	7	8	9
2	0	2	4	6	8	**10**	**12**	**14**	**16**	**18**
3	0	3	6	9	**12**	**15**	**18**	**21**	**24**	**27**
4	0	4	8	**12**	**16**	**20**	**24**	*28*	*32*	*36*
5	0	5	**10**	**15**	**20**	**25**	**30**	**35**	**40**	**45**
6	0	6	**12**	**18**	**24**	**30**	*36*	*42*	*48*	*54*
7	0	7	**14**	**21**	*28*	**35**	*42*	49	*56*	*63*
8	0	8	**16**	**24**	*32*	**40**	*48*	*56*	*64*	*72*
9	0	9	**18**	*27*	*36*	**45**	*54*	*63*	*72*	**81**

Let's check that its persistence is 4:

$77 \rightarrow 49 \rightarrow 36 \rightarrow 18 \rightarrow 8$

So the smallest consistent number is **77,** and the next one is, of course, **177.**

27. Eurocking Chairs

Let "abcd" be the price of the two chairs in deutsche marks. With the prices in DM and in FF being integers, and the official rate being 10 FF for 3 DM, we can say that the price in FF must be a multiple of 10, which means that *its* last digit must be a 0. And that digit can't be a, because a is the first digit of the price in DM, and the price in DM is a multiple of 3. Since the price is a multiple of 3 in DM, it is also a multiple of 3 in FF, since both prices have the same digits, only in a different order (remembering the trick for telling whether a number is divisible by 3).

So the price in DM must be a multiple of 9, since it is the price in FF $\times$ 3/10. Finally, since the price in FF is a four-digit number, its thousands digit can be 9 at the most, so "abcd" < 3,000 (since "abcd" is the price in DM).

From all that, we can say

- a = either 1 or 2.
- $a + b + c + d$ is a multiple of 9.
- either b, c, or d is 0.

Let's try $a = 2$. Then the price in DM is greater than or equal to 2,000, and the price in FF is greater than or equal to 2,000 $\times$ 10/3, that is, greater than 6,666. We must find a number with the digits 2, 0, x, and y, with $2 + x + y$ a multiple of 9 and $x > 7$, or $x = 6$ and $y \geq 6$. There are several solutions: 2,070, 2,079, 2,088 (not putting the digits in order).

Let's check all of them:

7,200 $\times$ 3/10 = 2,160	This solution doesn't fit, since the digits are not the same.
7,020 $\times$ 3/10 = 2,106	This solution doesn't fit either.
7,920 $\times$ 3/10 = 2,376	This solution doesn't fit either.
7,290 $\times$ 3/10 = 2,187	This solution doesn't fit either.
8,820 $\times$ 3/10 = 2,646	This solution doesn't fit either.
8,280 $\times$ 3/10 = 2,484	This solution doesn't fit either.

Now let's try $a = 1$. The price in FF must be greater than 3,333 and smaller than 6,667. There are several solutions: 1,035, 1,044, 1,062 (not putting the digits in order).

$3,510 \times 3/10 = 1,053$ **This solution does fit.**
$4,410 \times 3/10 = 1,323$ This solution doesn't fit, since the digits are not the same.
$4,140 \times 3/10 = 1,242$ This solution doesn't fit either.
$5,310 \times 3/10 = 1,593$ This solution doesn't fit either.
$5,130 \times 3/10 = 1,539$ This solution doesn't fit either.
$6,120 \times 3/10 = 1,836$ This solution doesn't fit either.
$6,210 \times 3/10 = 1,863$ This solution doesn't fit either.

Then the only solution is that the price is 3,510 FF or 1,053 DM.
Paying with bills of 500 FF, the change will be $4,000 - 3,510 = 490$ FF, that is, $490 \times 3/10 = 147$ DM, that is, $147/2 = $ **73.50 euros.**

28. The Remaining Cells

The regions labeled A through O in the Venn diagram represent the various possibilities of a number being a multiple of one or more of the numbers 4, 5, 7, and 13.

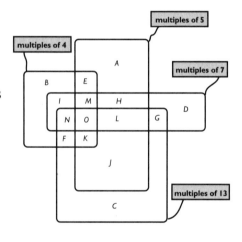

In that diagram, region O contains the numbers that are simultaneously multiples of those four numbers. Only one number fits: $4 \times 5 \times 7 \times 13 = 1,820$. In region M are the multiples of $4 \times 5 \times 7 = 140$, except for 1,820 (the number already counted in O): $14 - 1 = 13$

In region N are the multiples of $4 \times 7 \times 13 = 364$, except for 1,820: $5 - 1 = 4$

In region L are the multiples of $5 \times 7 \times 13 = 455$, except for 1,820: $4 - 1 = 3$

In K are the multiples of $4 \times 5 \times 13 = 260$, except for 1,820: $7 - 1 = 6$

In E are the multiples of $4 \times 5 = 20$, minus those that were found before:
$\ldots 99 - (13 + 6 + 1) = 79$

In I, multiples of $4 \times 7 = 28$, minus those that were found before:
$71 - (13 + 4 + 1) = 53$

In F, multiples of $4 \times 13 = 52$, minus those that were found before:
$38 - (6 + 4 + 1) = 27$

In *J*, multiples of $5 \times 13 = 65$, minus those that were found before:
$30 - (6 + 3 + 1) = 20$

In *G*, multiples of $7 \times 13 = 91$, minus those that were found before:
$21 - (4 + 3 + 1) = 13$

In *H*, multiples of $5 \times 7 = 35$, minus those that were found before:
$57 - (13 + 3 + 1) = 40$

In *A*, multiples of 5, minus those that were found before:
$399 - (79 + 40 + 20 + 13 + 6 + 3 + 1) = 237$

In *B*, multiples of 4, minus those that were found before:
$498 - (79 + 53 + 27 + 13 + 6 + 4 + 1) = 315$

In *C*, multiples of 13, minus those that were found before:
$153 - (27 + 20 + 13 + 6 + 4 + 3 + 1) = 79$

In *D*, multiples of 7, minus those that were found before:
$285 - (53 + 40 + 13 + 13 + 4 + 3 + 1) = 158$

So the total number of perforated cells is:
$1 + 13 + 4 + 3 + 6 + 79 + 53 + 27 + 20 + 13 + 40 + 237 + 315 + 79 + 158 = 1{,}048$

Then $1{,}995 - 1{,}048 = \textbf{947 cells}$ are left intact.

Note: This calculation of the number of cells is in fact the application of the *principle of inclusion-exclusion*: Let $A_1, A_2, \ldots, A_n$ be n sets. Then:

$$\left| \bigcup_{i=1}^{n} A_i \right| = \sum_{i=1}^{n} |A_i| - \sum_{1 \le i < j \le n} |A_i \cap A_j| + \sum_{1 \le i < j < k \le n} |A_i \cap A_j \cap A_k|$$
$$- \ldots + (-1)^{n+1} \left| \bigcap_{i=1}^{n} A_i \right|$$

29. Upside Down

Among the ten digits used in base 10, there are only seven digits that can be read upside down. These are 1 (its reflection is 1), 2 (its reflection is 5), 5 (its reflection is 2), 6 (its reflection is 9), 8 (its reflection is 8), 9 (its reflection is 6), and 0 (its reflection is 0).

Then writing in order the numbers that are readable upside down means writing in order only the numbers that use the digits belonging to the set (1, 2, 4, 6, 8, 9, 0). It's like writing all numbers in base 7, but using the symbols 1, 2, 5, 6, 8, 9, and 0, instead of the symbols 1, 2, 3, 4, 5, 6, and 0, which are usually used in base 7.

Let's convert 1,995 to base 7: $1,995 = 5 \times 7^3 + 5 \times 7^2 + 5 \times 7 + 0$

So 1,995 in base 7 is written 5,550.

But in the pseudo-base 7 that we are using, the digit 3 is replaced by 5, the digit 4 by 6, 5 by 8, and 6 by 9. So 5,550 will be written 8,880. Thus **8,880** is the 1,995th number that can be read upside down.

$$
\begin{array}{r|lr}
7 & 1,995 & \\
7 & 285 & +\ 0 \\
7 & 40 & +\ 5 \\
7 & 5 & +\ 5 \\
& 0 & +\ 5 \\
\end{array}
$$

30. Ring Fingers

First let's look at the blue hands.

The first number landing on the ring finger is 2. The next one is $2 + 10$. (We must count the 5 fingers on the right, and then come back on the 4 fingers closest to the ring finger.) In the same way, we see that the next number will be $12 + 2$, and so on. Thus the set of numbers corresponding to the blue ring finger is: $2, 2 + 10, 12 + 2, 14 + 10, 24 + 2, \ldots, 12n, 12n + 2, \ldots$

Now let's look at the green hands.

The first number landing on the ring finger is also 2. The next one is $2 + 12$. (We have to count the 6 fingers on the right, and then come back on the 5 fingers closest to the ring finger.) In the same way, we see that the next number will be $14 + 2$, and so on. So the set of numbers corresponding to the green ring finger is: $2, 2 + 12, 14 + 2, 16 + 12, 28 + 2, \ldots, 14n, 14n + 2, \ldots$

So we are looking for all the numbers that are at the same time:

- smaller than 1,996
- greater than 1,896
- of the form $12n$ or $12n + 2$
- of the form $14p$ or $14p + 2$

The table contains a list of these numbers. We can see that four numbers satisfy these conditions: **1,920, 1,932, 1,934,** and **1,946.**

$12n$	$12n + 2$	$14n$	$14n + 2$
1,896	1,898	1,904	1,906
1,908	1,910	1,918	**1,920**
1,920	1,922	**1,932**	**1,934**
1,932	**1,934**	**1,946**	1,948
1,944	**1,946**	1,960	1,962
1,956	1,958	1,974	1,976
1,968	1,970	1,988	1,990
1,980	1,982		
1,992	1,994		

31. Drive-Through

The number $x = 0.\text{COFFEECOFFEECOFFEE} \ldots$ is the infinite decimal expansion of COFFEE/999,999. (This is because $10^6 x = \text{COFFEE} + x$).

So we must have:
$$\frac{\text{COFFEE}}{999,999} = \frac{\text{FOCE}}{\text{VOLVO}}$$

VOLVO must be a divisor of $999,999 \times \text{FOCE}$.

Let's express 999,999 as a product of primes: $999,999 = 3^3 \times 7 \times 11 \times 13 \times 37$. Let's remember the rule of divisibility by 11: A number can be divided by 11 if the difference between the sum of its digits in the odd ranks and the sum of its digits in the even ranks is either zero or a multiple of 11.

Using this rule, we notice that VOLVO is congruent (modulo 11) to $(O + L + V) - (O + V) = L$. Also, COFFEE is congruent (modulo 11) to $(E + F + O) - (E + F + C) = O - C$. Since 999,999 is a multiple of 11, we have $L(O - C) \equiv 0 \bmod 11$, from which $L = 0$, since $O - C < 11$ and $O \neq C$.

So we have: $\text{VOLVO} = \text{VO 0 VO} = 1001 \times \text{VO} = 7 \times 11 \times 13 \times \text{VO}$

The only possible solutions are:

VO = 27, with $999,999 = 37 \times \text{VOLVO}$ and $\text{COFFEE} = 37 \times \text{FOCE}$
or VO = 37, with $999,999 = 27 \times \text{VOLVO}$ and $\text{COFFEE} = 27 \times \text{FOCE}$

In both cases, we must have $7 \times \text{E} \equiv \text{E} \bmod 11$. The only possible values for E are 0 or 5. Since 0 is already taken by L, E must be 5.

Let's first assume that VOLVO = 27027. C7FF55 = 37 × F7C5 means C = 3, which is impossible, or C = 1. This last solution leads to $174455 = 37 \times 4715$. Now let's suppose that VOLVO = 37037. C7FF55 = 27 × F7C5 means C = 2 or C = 1. These solutions lead to nothing.

So the only solution is **COFFEE = 174,455.**

32. The Nine Factors

First let's consider the problem without the signs. By expressing the absolute values of the products in prime factors, we see that the only possible position for 7 is i and for 5 is b. The digit 9 can only be at h or i, and with i being already occupied, the right position is h.

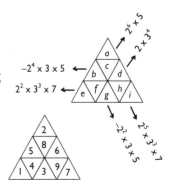

Then 3 or 6 can be at g, and 6 or 3 can be at d. But 2^4 is too big to go in c, so we have 8 in c, 6 in d, and 3 in g. We then place 4 in f, 1 in e, and 2 in a, which completes the triangle.

First method for calculating the signs:

Now let's consider the signs of the products. The table shows that when the signs of the factors *a, e,* and *i* are changed, the signs of the six products don't change.

It is the same if the signs of *b, d, f,* and *h* are changed. Moreover, those changes and their combinations are the only ones that keep the signs of all the products (except the identity).

All the **eight possible solutions** for the signs are shown here. Only the negative signs are shown. (See the triangle on the previous page for the numbers.)

Second method for calculating the signs:

Studying only the signs of the nine factors, with *x, y,* and *z* belonging to the set $\{-1, +1\}$, there is only one way to complete the figure to get the right products. So there are 2^3 solutions, that is, **eight solutions.**

Factors / Products	a	b	c	d	e	f	g	h	i	
bcd		*b*	*c*	*d*						< 0
bfg		*b*				*f*	*g*			< 0
efghi					*e*	*f*	*g*	*h*	*i*	> 0
abcef	*a*	*b*	*c*		*e*	*f*				> 0
dgh				*d*			*g*	*h*		> 0
acdhi	*a*		*c*	*d*				*h*	*i*	> 0
Number of occurrences	2	3	3	3	2	3	3	3	2	

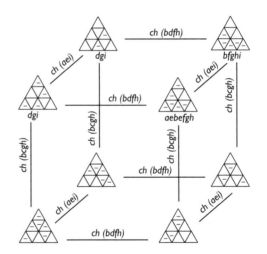

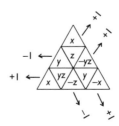

33. Red Light/Green Light

Signal A emits 5 beams in 6 minutes, not counting the first one, so there is a beam every 6/5 minutes. Signal B emits 32 beams in 31 minutes, not counting the first one, so there is a beam every 31/32 minutes.

Counting the first signals as 0, let's consider the xth signal of A and yth signal of B. They will coincide if $x \times 6/5 = y \times 31/32$. From that equation we get $y/x = (6/5) \times (32/31) = 192/155$.

So we can say that the 155th signal of A will coincide with the 192nd signal of B. Indeed, $155 \times 6/5 = 186$ and $192 \times 31/32 = 186$. Unfortunately, 186 minutes is 3 hours and 6 minutes, and Nina's observation time is much shorter. So we need to find the closest possible fraction to 192/155 with smaller terms.

Let's decompose 192/155 as a continued fraction. The method is shown on the left diagram, and the result appears on the right.

$$
\begin{array}{c}
\,1 \\
155\overline{)\,192} \\
-155 \\
\hline
37
\end{array}
\quad
\begin{array}{c}
\,4 \\
37\overline{)\,155} \\
-148 \\
\hline
7
\end{array}
\quad
\begin{array}{c}
\,5 \\
7\overline{)\,37} \\
-35 \\
\hline
2
\end{array}
\quad
\begin{array}{c}
\,3 \\
2\overline{)\,7} \\
-6 \\
\hline
1
\end{array}
\quad
\begin{array}{c}
\,2 \\
1\overline{)\,2} \\
-2 \\
\hline
0
\end{array}
\qquad
\frac{192}{155} = 1 + \cfrac{1}{4 + \cfrac{1}{5 + \cfrac{1}{3 + \cfrac{1}{2}}}}
$$

A shorthand notation for this continued fraction is $192/155 = \,< 1, 4, 5, 3, 2 >$.

The closest possible fraction would be written in this notation as $< 1, 4, 5, 3 >$. Let's calculate that fraction:
$5 + 1/3 = 16/3;\ 4 + 3/16 = 67/16;\ 1 + 16/67 = 83/67$

$$
1 + \cfrac{1}{4 + \cfrac{1}{5 + \cfrac{1}{3}}}
$$

This corresponds to A's **67th signal,** that is, after 80 minutes, 24 seconds $(67 \times 6/5 = 402/5)$, and B's **83rd signal,** that is, after 80 minutes, 24.375 seconds $(83 \times 31/32 = 2{,}573/32)$.

The difference between those two signals is **0.375 seconds.**

34. Closing Up Fractions

Let's decompose 225/157 as a continued fraction:

$$
\begin{array}{c}
\,1 \\
157\overline{)\,255} \\
-157 \\
\hline
68
\end{array}
\quad
\begin{array}{c}
\,2 \\
68\overline{)\,157} \\
-136 \\
\hline
21
\end{array}
\quad
\begin{array}{c}
\,3 \\
21\overline{)\,68} \\
-63 \\
\hline
5
\end{array}
\quad
\begin{array}{c}
\,4 \\
5\overline{)\,21} \\
-20 \\
\hline
1
\end{array}
\quad
\begin{array}{c}
\,5 \\
1\overline{)\,5} \\
-5 \\
\hline
0
\end{array}
\qquad
\frac{225}{157} = 1 + \cfrac{1}{2 + \cfrac{1}{3 + \cfrac{1}{4 + \frac{1}{5}}}}
$$

A shorthand notation for this continued fraction is $225/157 = \,< 1, 2, 3, 4, 5 >$.

Since the required fraction must be "close" without being equal to 225/157, its decomposition will be $< 1, 2, 3, 4, 5, k >$, with k determined by the other conditions.

The greater k is, the closer we get to 225/157. Indeed, $5 + (1/k)$ approaches 5.

Let's write $< 1, 2, 3, 4, 5, k >$ as a fraction (see box).

The conditions on the numerator N and the denominator D lead to $N - D \leq 1{,}995$, that is, $225k + 43 - 157k - 30 \leq 1{,}995$ or $68k \leq 1{,}982$, from which we get $k \leq 29$ (since k must be an integer).

$$5 + \frac{1}{k} = \frac{5k + 1}{k}$$

$$4 + \frac{k}{5k + 1} = \frac{21k + 4}{5k + 1}$$

$$3 + \frac{5k + 1}{21k + 4} = \frac{68k + 13}{21k + 4}$$

$$2 + \frac{21k + 4}{68k + 13} = \frac{157k + 30}{68k + 13}$$

$$1 + \frac{68k + 13}{157k + 30} = \frac{225k + 43}{157k + 30}$$

Replacing k with 29 leads to the fraction **6,568/4,583,** which will put an end to the duel. Note that $6{,}568/4{,}583 - 225/157 \approx 0.0000013979$. Using this method with $< 1, 2, 3, 4, 5, -k >$ leads to 6,482/4,523, which is not as close as the first.

35. The Multidivisible Cube

Call the original number in the problem n and let $d(n)$ be the number of its divisors.

If we decompose n into a product of prime factors, we can write $n = p_1^{r_1} \cdot p_2^{r_2} \cdots p_k^{r_k}$, where $p_1, p_2, \ldots, p_k$ are the prime factors and $r_1, r_2, \ldots, r_k$ are their respective exponents.

We have $d(n) = (r_1 + 1)(r_2 + 1) \cdots (r_k + 1)$, since each factor can appear in a divisor anywhere from 0 times (that is, as a "1") to as many times as it appears in n.

Similarly, since $n^3 = p_1^{3r_1} \cdot p_2^{3r_2} \cdots p_k^{3r_k}$, we have $d(n^3) = (3r_1 + 1)(3r_2 + 1) \cdots (3r_k + 1)$.

If n satisfies the conditions of the problem, we must have $(3r_1 + 1)(3r_2 + 1) \cdots (3r_k + 1) = 5(r_1 + 1)(r_2 + 1) \cdots (r_k + 1)$.

For $k = 1$, this becomes $3r_1 + 1 = 5(r_1 + 1)$, which leads to $r_1 = -2$, which is impossible.

Now $r \geq 1$ means that $3r_i + 1 \geq 2(r_i + 1)$ for all $i = 1, 2, \ldots, k$, so for $k \geq 3$ we have $(3r_1 + 1)(3r_2 + 1) \cdots (3r_k + 1) \geq 2^k(r_1 + 1)(r_2 + 1) \cdots (r_k + 1) > 5 (r_1 + 1)(r_2 + 1) \cdots (r_k + 1)$, contradicting the hypothesis.

The only remaining case is if $k = 2$. We then have $(3r_1 + 1)(3r_2 + 1) = 5(r_1 + 1)(r_2 + 1)$, which leads to $2r_1r_2 - r_1 - r_2 = 0$. From this equation, we get $r_2 = \frac{r_1 + 2}{2r_1 - 1}$. For $r_1 = 1$ this gives $r_2 = 3$; for $r_1 = 2$ we get a non-integer for r_2; for $r_1 = 3$ we get $r_2 = 1$; and for $r_1 > 3$ we get $1/2 < r_2 < 1$, so again r_2 is not an integer.

Thus the only allowable values are $\{r_1, r_2\} = \{1, 3\}$. The number of divisors of the square is then $d(n^2) = (2r_1 + 1)(2r_2 + 1) = 3 \cdot 7$ or $7 \cdot 3 = 21$.

The square of the original number has **21 divisors.**

36. Logoniversary

The first obvious element is that no course needs fewer turns than a spiral. There are other courses that use equally few turns, such as a zigzag that repeatedly goes from one edge of the grid all the way to the opposite edge, but there are no courses that need less.

Let's see how things look depending on whether n is even or odd.

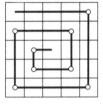
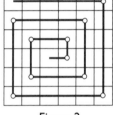

Figure I   Figure 2

- If n is odd, as in Figure 1, the left side of the grid has $n - 1$ turns, and so does the right side. $n^2 - 1 + 2(n - 1) = n^2 + 2n - 3$ keystrokes.
- If n is even, as in Figure 2, the left side of the grid has $n - 2$ turns and the right side has n turns. $n^2 - 1 + (n - 2) + n = n^2 + 2n - 3$ keystrokes.

So we're looking for a number that can be written $n^2 + 2n - 3$ and that is a plausible year for their wedding.

The table shows that the only solution is a 43×43 board. Ada and Charles were married in **1932.**

n	40	41	42	43	44	45
$n^2 + 2n - 3$	1677	1760	1845	**1932**	2021	2112

37. Raymond's Pond

There are 128 amphibians and only 113 tails, so there are 113 tadpoles and $128 - 113 = 15$ frogs.

Let x be the number of legless tadpoles, y the number of tadpoles with two legs, and z the number of tadpoles with four legs.

Raymond's census leads to the following equations:

$$\begin{cases} 2y + 4z + 60 = 264 \\ \quad x + y + z = 113 \end{cases} \quad \text{which leads to} \quad \begin{cases} \quad y + 2z = 102 \\ x + y + z = 113 \end{cases}$$

The fact that one category of tadpoles must be twice another forces us to study six possible situations:

1) $x = 2y$, 2) $y = 2x$, 3) $y = 2z$, 4) $z = 2y$, 5) $x = 2z$, 6) $z = 2x$

1. $(x = 2y)$: Replacing x with $2y$ and solving the equations leads to non-integer values of x, y, and z, which is impossible.
2. $(y = 2x)$: Replacing y with $2x$ leads to $x = 31$, $y = 62$, and $z = 20$.
3. $(y = 2z)$: Replacing y with $2z$ in the first equation leads to $z = 25.5$, which is impossible.
4. $(z = 2y)$: Replacing z with $2y$ in the first equation leads to $5y = 102$, which is also impossible.
5. $(x = 2z)$: Replacing x with $2z$ leads to $z = 11$, $x = 22$, and $y = 80$.
6. $(z = 2x)$: Replacing z with $2x$ leads to negative values of x and z, which is, of course, impossible.

So there are **two solutions:** Raymond has counted either **62 or 80 two-legged tadpoles.**

38. Statistics

Let h be the number of attendants in category HC, g the number in category GP, and l the number in category L1.

The data leads to the following equations:

$$2(0.1h + 0.5l + 0.4g) = 0.4h + 0.5l + 0.1g$$
$$h + l + g = 1{,}000$$

which leads to the equation $7l + 9g = 2{,}000$, for which we must have positive integer solutions.

The pair $(4, -3)$ is a particular solution for $7l + 9g = 1$, so $(8{,}000, -6{,}000)$ is a particular solution for $7l + 9g = 2{,}000$.

The general solution for this equation has to be $(8{,}000 - 9k, -6{,}000 + 7k)$ with $858 \le k \le 888$, so that both l and g will be positive numbers.

The possible values for g are 6, 13, 20, 27, 34, . . . , but $0.4g$ must be an integer, so not as many possible values fit:
20 ($k = 860$), 55 ($k = 865$), 90 ($k = 870$), 125 ($k = 875$), 160 ($k = 880$), 195 ($k = 885$)

Moreover, with $0.5l$ having to be an integer, l must be even, which eliminates some possible values of k: 865, 875, and 885.

Only three possibilities remain: $k = 960$, 870, or 880, which means that $g = 20$, 90, or 160, and $l = 260$, 170, or 80.

So there are **three solutions:** The number of L1 questionnaires is **80, 170, or 260.**

39. The Five Numbers

Let a, b, c, d, and e be the numbers written on the blackboard, and suppose that they are in ascending order: $a < b < c < d < e$.

These five numbers determine ten sums: $a + b$, $a + c$, $a + d$, $a + e$, $b + c$, $b + d$, $b + e$, $c + d$, $c + e$, $d + e$. The total is

$$4(a + b + c + d + e) = 6 + 7 + 8 + 8 + 9 + 9 + 10 + 10 + 11 + 12 = 90$$

so $a + b + c + d + e = 90/4 = 22.5$.

Moreover, $a + b$ and $a + c$ are the two smallest sums, while $c + e$ and $d + e$ are the greatest. So we have:

$$a + b = 6 \qquad a + c = 7 \qquad c + e = 11 \qquad d + e = 12$$

Then step by step, we conclude that $c = 22.5 - 6 - 12 = 4.5$, $a = 7 - 4.5 = 2.5$, $b = 6 - 2.5 = 3.5$, $e = 11 - 4.5 = 6.5$, and $d = 12 - 6.5 = 5.5$.

So the five numbers are: **2.5, 3.5, 4.5, 5.5, and 6.5.**

40. The Prophecy of Nostradaplus

This problem requires finding digits a, b, c, and d such that $10a + b + 10c + d = 10b + c$, which yields $10a + d = 9(b - c)$. $10a + d$ being greater than 0, we must have $b > c$. Let's try out all the possible values for $b - c$:

$b - c = 0$; then "ad" $= 0$. This doesn't work.

$b - c = 1$; then "ad" $= 9$. This doesn't work either.

$b - c = 2$; then "ad" $= 18$. Eight possible solutions: 1208, 1318, 1428, 1538, 1648, 1758, 1868, 1978

$b - c = 3$; then "ad" $= 27$. Seven possible solutions: 2307, 2417, 2527, 2637, 2747, 2857, 2967

$b - c = 4$; then "ad" $= 36$. Six possible solutions: 3406, 3516, 3626, 3736, 3846, 3956

$b - c = 5$; then "ad" $= 45$. Five possible solutions: 4505, 4615, 4725, 4835, 4945

$b - c = 6$; then "ad" $= 54$. Four possible solutions: 5604, 5714, 5824, 5934

$b - c = 7$; then "ad" $= 63$. Three possible solutions: 6703, 6813, 6923

$b - c = 8$; then "ad" $= 72$. Two possible solutions: 7802, 7912

$b - c = 9$; then "ad" $= 81$. One possible solution: 8901

So there are $8 + 7 + 6 + 5 + 4 + 3 + 2 + 1 = (8 \times 9)/2 = $ **36 major years,** and the next ones will be **2307 and 2417.**

41. Syldavian Exchanges

The data leads to the following equations:

$$\begin{cases} \dfrac{9}{z} = \dfrac{8}{y} + 1 \\[2mm] \dfrac{8}{x} = \dfrac{6}{z} + 2 \\[2mm] \dfrac{6}{x} = \dfrac{4}{y} + 2 \end{cases}$$

which can be simplified to:

$$\begin{cases} \dfrac{9}{z} = \dfrac{8}{y} + 1 & (1) \\[2mm] \dfrac{4}{x} = \dfrac{3}{z} + 1 & (2) \\[2mm] \dfrac{3}{x} = \dfrac{2}{y} + 1 & (3) \end{cases}$$

The three equations (1), (2), and (3) are indeterminate—they are not independent— but the requirement that the solutions be consecutive positive integers makes the solution unique.

Let's examine equation (3): $1 + (2/y) > 1$, hence $0 < x < 3$, that is, $x = 1$ or $x = 2$.
If $x = 1$, then $y = z = 1$, but x, y, and z must be consecutive integers.
If $x = 2$, then $y = 4$, and $z = 3$. This possibility fits the conditions.

Exchanging (at the official rate) one Syldavian crown for stamps, another one for corks, and a last one for cards enables us to get $2 + 3 + 4 = $ **9 items.**

50 Mathematical Puzzles and Problems ◆ Red Collection
©2001 Key Curriculum Press

42. The Golf Ball

The golf ball is just like a polyhedron whose faces are hexagons and pentagons.

Let p be the number of pentagons. Then the polyhedron has $(384 - p)$ hexagons. Each and every vertex is the intersection of three faces, since the dimples are arranged as triangles.

Let V be the number of vertices. Then $V = 5p/3 + 6(384 - p)/3$ (since numbering the vertices of each polygon means counting each vertex of the polyhedron three times).

Also, each edge is the intersection of two faces.

So if we let E be the number of edges, $E = 5p/2 + 6(384 - p)/2$.

The numbers F, V, and E of faces, vertices, and edges of a polyhedron (without "holes") are constrained by Euler's Theorem: $V + F - E = 2$.

For our golf ball, that means: $5p/3 + 2(384 - p) + 384 - 5p/2 - 3(384 - p) = 2$. This equation has the solution $p = 12$.

So there are **12 dimples** that are surrounded by only 5 others.

43. Memorization

Let N be the code number.

Then $N +$ "$1N1$" $= 100 \times N$
Write down the following addition:

```
  . . . . . . . . . .  .
+ . . . . . . . . . .  . 1
 ─────────────────────────
  . . . . . . . . .  . 0 0
```

From right to left, in each column there is only one solution. But with each step, we must check whether or not a 1 could be added on the left.

```
  . . . . . .  9          . . . . .  0 9
+ . . . . . .  9 1      + . . . .  0 9 1
 ───────────────         ─────────────────
  . . . . .  9 0 0        . . .  0 9 0 0
```

$$1\ 1\ 2\ 3\ 5\ 9\ 5\ 5\ 0\ 5\ 6\ 1\ 7\ 9\ 7\ 7\ 5\ 2\ 8\ 0\ 9$$
$$+\ \mathbf{1}\ 1\ 1\ 2\ 3\ 5\ 9\ 5\ 5\ 0\ 5\ 6\ 1\ 7\ 9\ 7\ 7\ 5\ 2\ 8\ 0\ 9\ \mathbf{1}$$
$$\overline{}$$
$$1\ 1\ 2\ 3\ 5\ 9\ 5\ 5\ 0\ 5\ 6\ 1\ 7\ 9\ 7\ 7\ 5\ 2\ 8\ 0\ 9\ \mathbf{0}\ \mathbf{0}$$

As shown above, the addition can be ended after having written 21 digits.

So the code number is 112,359,550,561,797,752,809 and the sum of its digits is **97**.

Alternative method:

Let N be the code number and n the number of digits in N's decimal form.

From the data

$$10^{n+1} + 10N + 1 = 99N, \text{ that is, } 10^{n+1} + 1 = 89N$$

From this equation, N is the quotient by 89 of the smallest possible number that can be written 1000 . . . 001, and which is divisible by 89. So N is one more than the integer part of the quotient by 89 of the smallest possible power of ten congruent to 88 modulo 89.

That quotient can be found by writing down the division $89\overline{)100000\ldots}$ and calculating it until the remainder is 88.

$$
\begin{array}{r}
112{,}359{,}550{,}561{,}797{,}752{,}808 \\
89\overline{)10{,}000{,}000{,}000{,}000{,}000{,}000{,}000} \\
\underline{89} \\
110 \\
\underline{89} \\
210 \\
\underline{178} \\
320 \\
\end{array}
$$

(many steps left out . . .)

$$
\begin{array}{r}
800 \\
\underline{712} \\
88
\end{array}
$$

Once that calculation is done, we see that $N = 112{,}359{,}550{,}561{,}797{,}752{,}808 + 1$. So the code number is 112,359,550,561,797,752,809 and the sum of its digits is **97**.

44. Stepping Stones

Let P be the box that has no stones left for Matthew to take, and let Q, R, and S be the successively preceding boxes, in the order set by the game. Q contains at least three stones from the previous moves from boxes R, S, and P. For Q to have four stones, it would have to have gotten at least two stones on one of those moves. But then on that same move, P would have received at least one stone, and it would not be empty now. So Q contains exactly three stones. The same reasoning shows that R, after having been emptied, got only one stone from the previous moves from S and P, so it now contains two stones.

Similarly, S, after having been emptied, got only one stone from the move from P. When Matthew stops playing, he has exactly $3 + 2 + 1 =$ **6 stones left.**

45. Lucky's Race

The traffic lights simultaneously turn green every 50 seconds, and they can be passed only during the first 30 seconds of those 50-second intervals (instant 0 and instant 30 included).

Each time Lucky goes 500 m, it takes her 74 seconds, that is, $50 + 24$ seconds. So the state of the traffic lights will be advanced by 24 seconds.

Let's suppose that Lucky starts from a light x seconds after it has turned green (see first column in table below), and let's use the table to study the state of the following lights. In each case, the table shows the number of seconds since the light last turned green.

1st light	2nd light	3rd light	4th light	5th light	6th light	7th light	8th light	9th light
0	24	48						
2	26	0	24	48				
4	28	2	26	0	24	48		
6	30	4	28	2	26	0	24	48
26	0	24	48					
28	2	26	0	24	48			

If Lucky starts from a traffic light at the precise moment when it turns green, then we see in the first row of the table that she'll encounter the 3rd light red (it has been that color for 18 seconds, and will stay so 2 more seconds).

So she should have started at least 2 seconds later to be able to pass the 3rd light at the moment it turns green. But now she'll get to the 5th light when it's red, and she will also have to wait for 2 seconds. To be able to pass this 5th light, she should have started another 2 seconds later (third row). On every odd numbered light, she's stopped for 2 seconds. But now it's the 7th light that will be red when she gets there. If she starts yet another 2 seconds later (fourth row), she passes the 7th light but gets stuck at the 9th. If she leaves more than 6 seconds (and, as we will see, less than 26 seconds) after the 1st light has turned green, the 2nd light will be red when she gets there (not shown on the table). If she leaves 26 or 27 seconds after the 1st light has turned green, she'll be able to pass the 2nd light, but now the 4th light will be red (fifth row). If she waits 28 or 29 seconds, the 6th light is red (last row), and if she waits 30 seconds, that is, she starts just as the 1st light turns red, she gets caught at the 8th light (not shown). Finally, if she waits more than 30 seconds but less than 50 seconds, she can't even leave the 1st light, since it's already red.

So the most lights she can pass without stopping is **8,** by waiting 6 seconds to start.

46. The Four Letters

Each letter in the word will appear one more time than it already appears. So count the current number of appearances of each letter and see which appear once, twice, three times, or four times, and see which words can be made from them (in the order specified).

E and S cannot be among the added letters, because they already appear eight times and six times respectively. J, K, M, P, Q, X, Y, and Z don't appear at all. We have B, D, G, L, U, V, and W already appearing once (so that one of them would appear twice if it were one of the added letters), A, C, F, H, and O appearing twice, R appearing three times, and I, N, and T appearing four times.

Of the words that can be formed using the letters in that order, namely BARN, BORN, DART, LORN, WARN, WART, WORN, and WORT, the only one that can be thrown is a **DART.**

47. Knossos

Let's call a portion of wall that is the length of a grid cell (10 m) a "panel." Every cell can have at least two panels, still leaving an entrance and an exit to that cell. A cell cannot have four panels, or it would be isolated. For every cell that has three panels and is therefore a cul-de-sac (dead end), a little experimentation with drawing mazes will show that another cell somewhere must have only one panel, so that those two cells between them still average two panels per cell.

Since there are $6 \times 10 = 60$ cells, the maximum possible number of panels is $2 \times 60 = 120$—except that in the interior of the labyrinth, every panel is shared by two adjacent cells, so we have double-counted some of the panels. There are 30 exterior panels, so we have double-counted $120 - 30 = 90$ panels. We should have counted them as only 45 panels. Those, plus the 30 exterior panels, make a maximum possible total of 75 panels.

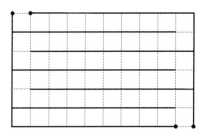

The figure shows that it is actually possible to achieve this maximum value. The maximum total length of the walls is $75 \times 10 = \textbf{750 m.}$

48. Traffic Lights

The maximum possible value is **23.** A possible solution is GGYGYYYGRRGRRRRGRRYRYGY.

This answer can be found by using what is called "backtracking," in which you keep guessing lights in an orderly way, always checking whether each guess is allowed by the rules, changing it to the next color if not, rechecking, and going back one guess to revise that guess if no more colors are allowed for the light you're currently guessing. You continue to proceed like that—guessing and checking, going on to the next light if the guess is acceptable, changing the guess if it is not, and going backward if there are no more possible guesses. You continue until there are no more possible guesses left for the very first light. There are many refinements that can speed up the process somewhat. For example, when you guess each light, you can mark off on all future lights the possible choices that your new guess has just eliminated.

49. Getting Even

In this type of problem, the solution can be found by starting at the end.

First consider some notation. The position (odd even 22) means that your opponent has an odd number of pawns, you have an even number, there are 22 pawns left, and it is your opponent's turn to move (all positions except the starting position will always be shown just before your opponent's move). Notice that since there is always an odd total number of pawns, any position must have either two evens and one odd, or three odds (including the number of pieces left), and notice that the winning position for you is (odd even 0). The double move (1 3) means that your opponent takes one pawn, then you take three pawns. Whatever move your opponent chooses, you will choose yours based on his move and the current position.

Near the end of the game, when it is your opponent's turn to move, you would like to be in either (even odd 6) or (even even 7). The figure shows why. Let's look at the situation one and two double moves before this.

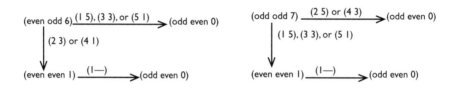

Extending this scenario backward, we can see that winning positions always have one of the forms (odd even (even multiple of 6)), (even odd (odd multiple of 6)), (even even (even multiple of 6) + 1), or (odd odd (odd multiple of 6) + 1). From positions (even odd (any multiple of 6)) the winning moves are (1 5), (2 3), (3 3), (4 1), or (5 1), and from positions (even odd (any multiple of 6) + 1) the winning moves are (1 5), (2 5), (3 3), (4 3), or (5 1).

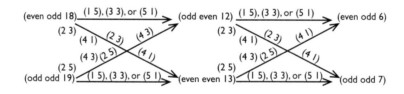

All that remains is to analyze the starting position and see which move of yours would guarantee a winning position. At the start, the position is $(0\ 0\ 1{,}995) = (\text{even even } 332 \cdot 6 + 3) = (\text{even even } [(\text{even multiple of 6}) + 1] + 2)$. So if you take two pawns, the position will be (even even (even multiple of 6) + 1), a winning position.

Therefore **you are guaranteed a win by taking two pawns on your first move.**

50. Scrooge's Ingots

Based on the conditions, we can conclude that
$D + (E + F + G) = D + (A + B + C) = A + (B + C + D) = A + (G + H + I)$.
So if we let a, b, c, d, e, f, g, h, and i be the respective lengths of the sides of A, B, C, D, E, F, G, H, and I's bases, the problem becomes equivalent to placing numbers from 1 to 9 in a triangle, while fulfilling these requirements:

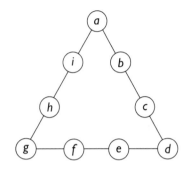

- The sum of the squares of the numbers of each side must be constant (call it k).
- The numbers on the vertices a, d, and g must be in ascending order.
- The two middle numbers on each side must be in ascending order, reading clockwise.

Adding up all the numbers on each side (which means that a, d, and g will be counted twice) leads to the following equation:

$$a^2 + d^2 + g^2 + (1^2 + 2^2 + 3^2 + 4^2 + 5^2 + 6^2 + 7^2 + 8^2 + 9^2) = 3k$$

$$(a^2 + d^2 + g^2)/3 + 95 = k$$

So we must have $a^2 + d^2 + g^2 \equiv 0 \bmod 3$ and $a^2 + b^2 + c^2 + d^2 = k \equiv 2 \bmod 3$ (and similarly for the other two sides).

Studying congruence modulo 3, we find that 3, 6, and 9 either are *all* vertices or *none* of them are vertices—and in fact, they are all on different sides. This is because any square is divisible either by 3 or by (a multiple of 3) + 1.

If 3, 6, and 9 are located at the vertices, then $k = 137$. On the side that has 3 and 6 for its vertices, the sum of the two missing squares must be $137 - 9 - 36 = 92$, which is impossible. So 3, 6, and 9 must be on three different sides.

Let's temporarily ignore the condition about the order of the middle two points on each side, and assume that 3, 6, and 9 are (in some permutation) the points b, e, and h. Once we find a solution, we can rearrange b and c, or e and f, or h and i as necessary. Let's examine the various permutations.

Case 1: $(b, e, h) = (3, 6, 9)$. Then $3^2 + c^2 + d^2 = g^2 + 9^2 + i^2 \Rightarrow c^2 + d^2 = g^2 + i^2 + 72 \geq 4^2 + 1^2 + 72 = 89 \Rightarrow c^2 \geq 89 - d^2$. The only allowable values for (c, d) are $(8, 5)$ and $(8, 7)$. If $(c, d) = (8, 5)$, then $8^2 + 5^2 = g^2 + i^2 + 72 \Rightarrow g^2 + i^2 = 17$, for which the only solution is $(g, i) = (4, 1)$, which forces $a = 2$, which forces $f = 7$. But then the sums of the squares along the sides are not equal. If $(c, d) = (8, 7)$, then $8^2 + 7^2 = g^2 + i^2 + 72 \Rightarrow g^2 + i^2 = 41$, so $(g, i) = (4, 5)$ or $(5, 4)$, in both of which cases (a, f) can be either $(1, 2)$ or $(2, 1)$. In all four combinations, once again the sums of the squares are not equal.

Case 2: $(b, e, h) = (3, 9, 6)$. Now we use $a^2 + 3^2 + c^2 = 9^2 + f^2 + g^2 \Rightarrow c^2 \geq 89 - a^2$. This time the only allowable value for (a, c) is $(5, 8)$, which means $(f, g) = (1, 4)$, which means $(d, i) = (2, 7)$ or $(7, 2)$. But in both cases, the sums of the squares are still not equal.

Case 3: $(b, e, h) = (6, 3, 9)$. This time $d^2 + 3^2 + f^2 = 9^2 + i^2 + a^2 \Rightarrow e^2 \geq 74 - d^2 \Rightarrow (d, f) = (4, 5), (5, 7), (5, 8), (7, 5)$, or $(7, 8)$. But $(4, 5)$ leads to $i^2 + a^2 = -31$, and $(5, 7)$ or $(7, 5)$ lead to $i^2 + a^2 = 2$, both of which are impossible. Now $(5, 8) \Rightarrow (a, i) = (1, 4)$ or $(4, 1)$ and $(c, g) = (2, 7)$, but once again, the sums of the squares are not equal in either case. And $(7, 8) \Rightarrow (a, i) = (4, 5)$ or $(5, 4)$, which leaves no allowable value for g.

We continue this way for the remaining cases $(6, 9, 3)$, $(9, 3, 6)$, and $(9, 6, 3)$, always equating the three values from the sides that have the 3 and the 9 in order to eliminate as many possibilities as quickly as we can. We discover that the only case that works is $(b, e, h) = (9, 6, 3)$. Here $g^2 + 3^2 + i^2 = 9^2 + c^2 + d^2 \Rightarrow i^2 \geq 77 - g^2 \Rightarrow (g, i) = (4, 8), (5, 8), (7, 8), (8, 4), (8, 5)$, or $(8, 7)$. Both $(4, 8)$ and $(8, 4)$ lead to $c^2 + d^2 = 8$, which is impossible. Both $(5, 8)$ and $(8, 5) \Rightarrow (c, d) = (1, 4)$ and $(a, f) = (2, 7)$, but neither makes the sums of the squares equal. Both $(7, 8)$ and $(8, 7) \Rightarrow (c, d) = (4, 5)$ or $(5, 4)$ and $(a, f) = (1, 2)$ or $(2, 1)$, but of the eight resulting possibilities, only $(a, c, d, f, g, i) = (2, 4, 5, 1, 8, 7)$ works.

Finally, making sure (b, c), (e, f), and (h, i) have the proper order, we have the **only possible solution** for the respective lengths of the nine sides:

A	B	C	D	E	F	G	H	I
2	4	9	5	1	6	8	3	7